How to Manage Troublesome Thoughts and Feelings:

Name It, Share It, Replace It

Mattie Slattery

How to Manage Troublesome Thoughts and Feelings: Name It, Share It, Replace It

Copyright © Mattie Slattery, 2021

The author has asserted his moral rights

First Published in 2021 by Feakle Street Publishing

ISBN: 978-1-8384087-0-1

A CIP Catalogue record for this book is available from the National Library

Typesetting, page design and layout by DocumentsandManuscripts.com

Cover design by Karolina Smorczewska

Published with the assistance of **The Manuscript Publisher**, publishing solutions for the digital age – www.TheManuscriptPublisher.com

How to Manage Troublesome Thoughts and Feelings:
Name It, Share It, Replace It

Copyright © Mattie Slattery, 2021

Publisher's Note

This book is not intended as an alternative to seeking therapy or professional help for a suspected or diagnosed mental health condition.

Dedication

To all who long for peace of mind and happiness:
family, loved ones, friends and fellow travellers on the
spiritual path...

Feeling, Attitude, Thought, Emotion

Name it...

Share it...

Replace it...

Foreword

I first learned about '*name it, share it, replace it*' as an approach to managing thoughts and feelings when speaking with the author about how to deal with a fear of flying. This book is for anyone who would like ideas about how to cope with worries or difficult feelings. It is divided into two main sections. The first describes a series of techniques that can promote happiness, peace of mind and well-being. The second explains how these techniques can be further enhanced, by exploring and considering our human faculties that go beyond the capabilities of the mind and body – our capacity to know.

The contents of this book could not be timelier and more relevant to the world that we live in today. At the time of writing, in January 2021, we are living with the threat posed by the COVID-19 global pandemic. As a result, collectively we are facing new challenges to all aspects of our lives; modifying our behaviour and human connection in ways that could not have been imagined a year ago. This book provides guidance and the rationale for a practice which, if adopted regularly, has the potential to facilitate coping with past, present and future challenges, as well as adversity, with clear and simple steps.

The author presents the reader with more than techniques for managing thoughts and emotions. In addition, the reader is encouraged to consider information that is aimed at empowering the individual towards a new way of life in terms of self-management of one's thoughts, emotions and how to interpret and work through difficult experiences.

On a journey towards greater well-being, happiness and peace of mind, the reader is invited to become more curious about their own mind, with three practical steps that relate to how to manage and regulate troublesome thoughts and emotions, when they arrive in-the-moment. The author has used these techniques extensively in his work as a personal development practitioner over 30 years, where he has worked with individuals and groups from all walks of life and observed many positive transformations.

The final section of the book moves on to present a new way of thinking about what a human is capable of. As humans, we will all experience troublesome thoughts and feelings, at least from time to time. The author describes the importance of tuning into the wisdom of our soul as a way to support and maintain our well-being, which goes beyond the initial practices outlined in the earlier chapters of the book.

Dr Sarah Jane Besser, Psychologist

Introduction

Happiness, peace of mind and an ever-deepening sense of calm and well-being are the hallmarks of those who have mastered the ability to manage their own thoughts and feelings.

It is reasonable to say that these characteristics are at the heart of what most human beings desire for themselves and their loved ones. If you would like these characteristics and qualities to be the hallmark of your life, then this book is for you.

In these pages, you will be introduced to a number of simple ideas and suggestions in the form of steps, stages and more. If you follow these suggestions, you will be taking your first steps to having happiness and peace of mind in your life permanently.

How and Why

In this approach to well-being, each of the suggestions takes only minutes to learn and seconds to apply. However, understanding how and why they work will take a little bit of time and perseverance. This involves acquiring knowledge and developing wisdom.

To achieve this goal you will be introduced to ways of cultivating these characteristics. This will allow a growing sense of well-being to become the mainstay of your life.

Once you start applying the suggestions, the benefits will be immediate and permanent, if you stick with it. It may take a little time for you to become aware of some of the benefits: it is sometimes the case that others become aware of the changes in your life before you become aware of them yourself.

Benefits

The level of benefit and results you achieve depend only on how much you want a better quality of life. Your happiness, peace of mind and well-being will be in direct proportion to your desire for and your willingness to change. In other words, the results you achieve will be exactly as you want them to be.

Best Wishes

Mattie Slattery

Jan 2021

Contents

CHAPTER ONE

The General Idea

This is a straightforward, no-frills approach towards a greater feeling of well-being, happiness and peace of mind. It is one approach of many. For the purpose of this book well-being, happiness and peace of mind are all about knowing that you are safe and secure in your life. It is that feeling of comfort and security you get when you are at peace with yourself and the world around you. It is being aware that all is well, even when things appear to be going against you. It is a feeling of peace and contentment that is with you at all times and under all conditions. You will begin to feel some of these benefits the moment you start to practise the first exercise sincerely. If you are open-minded and patient with yourself, you will be amazed at your progress right from the start.

Is it Possible?

Is this kind of well-being and happiness possible? Not alone is it possible but it is very simple to achieve. The approach presented here will give you the tools you need to move towards these higher levels of peace, happiness and well-being. However, you will need to have at least a basic knowledge of how and why these tools work. This is the minimum you will require to allow peace of mind, happiness and greater well-being to become permanent in your life. It is very simple to achieve this level of well-being and if you are willing to follow this approach, you will not be disappointed.

Simplify!

Human beings have been searching for a path to real happiness and peace of mind ever since mankind began to think, talk and feel. This search has brought volumes of research and books into being on this subject. Unfortunately, one of the unintended consequences of all this research and study is the over complication of what is actually a very simple process. So simple in fact that it is almost always overlooked by researchers and experts alike.

Humanity appears to have arrived at a point in time where it is almost impossible to find a simple approach to real happiness that actually works. So, one of the first things to take on board, as you explore *this approach* to well-being is that the steps you take will always remain simple. This will allow them to become woven into the fabric of your life through practice, without too much inconvenience to you.

To get the full benefit of what you are actually doing you will still need some basic information and understanding of what you are doing and why. In this book, essential information and suggestions are provided. These essentials are condensed into simple steps and exercises throughout for practical application. Your understanding will come from the practice of the suggestions and the ensuing discussions. This is the minimum you will need if you want to awaken your spirit and ensure your peace of mind and happiness.

Three Steps

When the idea of finding and developing an approach to peace of mind and happiness first surfaced, it was obvious that it needed to be both simple and effective. It was also clear that peace of mind and happiness were unachievable unless feelings, attitudes, thoughts and emotions could be managed. After exploring a number of therapies and self-help groups, all who provide great support in the field of mental health and, many years involved in personal development and adult education, the following steps were adapted and developed. There were three steps in the original approach.

The original steps:

- Acknowledge it
- Share it
- Kick it

These have evolved over the years to become:

- Name it
- Share it
- Replace it

Don't Take My Word

These steps are not the whole approach but they are at the core of how it works. Also, this approach has been used very effectively over the years, since its inception but, don't take my word for it. Try them out for yourself. If you decide to do so, you will need to try them out over a reasonable period of time: for example, six months to a year. Otherwise, all that will happen is you will get a short break from your troublesome thoughts and feelings then, they will come back again.

Once you start applying the steps and the other suggestions in this approach, you will need to continue doing so if you want to continue having freedom from troublesome thoughts and feelings permanently. The good news is that these steps and the other suggestions are simple and non-invasive. This means they will not interfere with your life to any great extent, except to allow happiness and peace of mind to become part of your being.

Learn in Minutes, Lasts a Lifetime

The three steps – name it, share it, replace it – are very simple to learn and easy to use. This is important because, as they are the core of the whole approach, they need to actually work and be simple enough to fit into your life. They can be committed to memory in minutes but will continue working for the rest of your life. To work them, all you have to do is practise them until you are using them spontaneously. They can be applied in seconds anywhere, anytime no matter what your work or profession. It is important to keep in mind that the steps are central to this approach and therefore essential to transforming your life.

Shared Experience and Action

Quotations from other authors have been avoided as much as possible to avoid turning this book into an academic exercise although, there are some references to other authors. Mostly, what is actually happening throughout these discussions is a sharing of experiences. Remember this! It is in the sharing of your experience that gives this approach to well-being its real power. It has to be experienced to get the full benefit. If you want happiness and peace of mind in your life, it is not enough to read about it and collect information or store knowledge. You must apply what you know to experience the benefits.

Practical Guide to Progress

The book is essentially a guide to quickly developing happiness and peace of mind. It has been designed for practical use. The Quick Guide will take you through the three core steps and get you started immediately on your journey. This is followed, later on, by essential, more in-depth discussions on the steps, how they function and what you will experience when you practise them. Remember the information and suggestions here are the minimum you will need to enjoy a contented peaceful life.

Progress is Unlimited

There is a lot of information in these pages but it is all condensed in the exercises so that you can start practising immediately. It is unlikely that you will take it all in the first time you read through therefore, you will probably need to refer to this book often especially in the early stages of your progress. As you set out on this part of your journey in life, be patient with yourself. Remember, your progress is unlimited and although you can awaken to the benefits of this new way of living instantly, the awakening is also unlimited. This means that you cannot make a parcel of your progress or arrive at some level and remain there. While you are using this approach, you will always be on the path of never-ending progress and advancement.

Never-Ending Progress

Keep in mind that nothing is perfect in the material world. Everything is in a state of perpetual development, changing, moving and advancing towards perfection. This means that nothing is motionless and as you know, it is difficult to stand still on something that keeps moving. Therefore you may fall a few times during your journey. The difference is now you know that falling is part of your progress. Once you realise and accept that it is okay to fall you will find it easier to get up and try again.

So remember, since there is nothing perfect in the material world, you will always be in a continuous state of progress and development. This will involve falling down and getting up and trying again maybe many times. This is why you will need a reference point such as this book to help you get up after a fall. This will allow you to continue your never-ending journey of progress in peace and contentment.

You

This book is written with you in mind. As you read through, you may notice that the word "you" is mentioned often. That is because this book is about you. It is all about your happiness, well-being and peace of mind. It does not matter what other people think. It is you who has the experience of your life and it is you who must navigate your way forward. On this journey, you will not be alone. You will meet many more on the road to peace of mind and happiness once you make a start.

Steps Stages and More

Once you have begun your journey using this approach to life, you will take a number of steps that will, in turn, take you through different stages. The steps will show you how to manage your thoughts and feelings as you make your way through the different stages of your life. Some of these stages will be discussed and explained so that you are aware of what is happening as you grow through them. If you stick with it, you will discover how to have happiness and peace of mind flowing into your life continuously.

2021

As the world came to the end of one decade with the passing of 2020 and began another, unhappiness, loneliness, anxiety, depression, active addictions, self-harm and suicide are among many other unpleasant human conditions in need of urgent attention. The arrival of the COVID-19 pandemic has made the overall condition of the world appear very bleak for many. As difficult as this situation is, it will pass because ultimately, every sickness can be healed and every question can be answered.

Therefore, although these are very trying times, they will end and no doubt, they will be replaced by other challenges for humanity. However, there will also be many opportunities and possibilities. On a personal level, these times can be used as an opportunity to restart your own life and turn your world into a place of peace and contentment, for you and your loved ones. The suggestions in this book offer a chance to begin this process but, it can only start with you. If you pursue this possibility, it will, first of all, improve your life then, make its way through your family and eventually, out into the wider community.

Caution! Warning!

This approach should not be used in place of other remedies that you may be using, except on the advice of your doctor. As mentioned at the beginning of this book:

"This book is not intended as an alternative to seeking therapy or professional help for a suspected or diagnosed mental health condition."

The motto of this approach is "as well as…" never, "instead of…"

The exercises in this approach to managing your thoughts and feelings will compliment any other form of therapeutic remedy you may be using at the moment. It is always good practice to seek out suitably qualified therapists and physicians who are willing to work in collaboration with you in all matters relating to your physical, mental and spiritual health. This approach has its foundation in the fundamentals of basic human fellowship and respect for all and in particular, respect for yourself.

Book Layout

There is quite a bit of information in these pages but it is laid out so that the material you need is easily accessible. However, if you happen to be stressed out or dealing with troublesome thoughts and feelings the last thing you will want to do is wade through endless pages of text. This book is written with this in mind and is designed to be a practical guide for those who seek peace of mind and contentment.

Therefore although there are twenty-two chapters in this book, they are made up of a number of short sections, subsections and paragraphs most of these have headings. This will make it easier to find and work through the material you need most at any particular time. The index of terms and topics at the back will give you a detailed snapshot of the content and also assist you in finding what you are looking for quickly.

Getting Started

You will not have to go through everything in these pages before you begin to feel the benefits of this approach to well-being but you will have to use the quick guide. You will find the quick guide in the next chapter to help get you started immediately. The moment that you begin to practise the exercises, you will be rewarded. However for the benefits to be permanent, you will need to continue practising and working your way through the rest of the material.

If you are not a "reader" as such, don't worry, as mentioned in the previous section, this book is written with you in mind. It is put together in chunks of information for easy access to what you need to know. In other words, short, easy-to-read paragraphs with as little jargon as possible.

You do not have to read through the entire book all at once. If you do, that's okay. Just remember, when you begin to practise the exercises, you must first go to the Quick Guide and learn how to practise the three core steps. Everyone will have their own idea on how they approach their own learning. Do what works best for you.

New Way of Life

You are about to set off on a journey into a new way of life, some of which may be familiar to you but some of it will not. Therefore it will be necessary to refer to this book often at least until you have memorised the practices. You also need to be aware that as you begin to feel better you will find yourself going back and forth between the old and the new way of living for a while. This is not unusual but it is why you will need to practise often, especially in the early stages. Once you keep practising, your new way of life will become established quickly.

Obviously, you will not be able to read through this book in seconds but, this does not take away from the fact that you can practise the steps and other exercises in seconds. All the exercises can be memorised in minutes and applied in seconds. Even the longer meditations can be practised in under thirty seconds and lengthened later if you wish.

The best way to go about this approach to well-being is to start slow and steady. Practise for a few seconds often, during the day. In this way, you will make steady progress.

You are now about to enter a wonderful new way of living in peace and happiness. You will not be alone on this journey. According to the law of attraction, when you begin, you will start to recognise and attract others who are also seeking a path to greater well-being.

CHAPTER TWO

Quick Guide to Getting Started

In this chapter, you will discover how to apply the three core steps of this approach so that you can get started on your journey immediately. First, you will discover how to apply the steps to fear then, you will be able to go on and apply them to any other thoughts and feelings you may want to let go of.

The steps can be memorised in minutes and applied in seconds. This will make it possible for you to use them anytime and in any place. In this chapter you will also be introduced to the idea of using helplines to practise sharing which is the engine of the steps. In later chapters, the steps will be discussed in greater detail but for now, all you need to know is how to apply them.

The Three Steps

> Name it
> Share it
> Replace it

How they Work

The simplest and best way to show how the steps work is by way of example. In this example, you will discover how to deal with fear but to do this, you will first need to know what fear actually is. For the purpose of this book, fear is defined simply as a troublesome feeling you get when you think or believe something bad is happening or is going to happen. Fear can be divided into two kinds: rational fear and irrational fear.

Rational Fear

Rational fear is the fear that helps to protect you and is essential for your survival. For example, fear of crocodiles. In this case, your rational fear will help you stay safe and far away from crocodiles. The steps will also help you manage this kind of fear.

Irrational Fear

Irrational fear is a form of fear that can make your life completely miserable if it is not dealt with. For example, fear of the dark. The three steps are used in exactly the same way for both types of fear.

Dealing with Fear

In this example, you will be dealing with an irrational fear of the dark. To manage this fear, you must first name it, then share it and finally, replace it as follows:

> **Name it** (to self): *I am afraid of the dark. I now let go of this fear.*
> **Share it** (self and other): *I am afraid of the dark. I now let go of this fear.*
> **Replace it** (to self): *I am safe and secure at all times and under all conditions.* Repeat three times.

Note!

When repeating step three, pause for a couple of seconds between repetitions. Be specific when you name a thought or feeling. When you first start to practise the steps use the same words in steps one and two. In step two, although you will ultimately be sharing with another, the first person you share with will always be yourself. Practise the three steps often throughout the day.

***

Another Way to Practise

As you can see, this is a very simple process and in the above exercise, everything takes place in your mind except when sharing with another person. Another way to practise the steps is to write down the feelings or thoughts that you are dealing with. Writing can help bring clarity to the practice of the steps. Along with giving you an additional way to communicate your thoughts and feelings, writing will also let you see a tangible expression of what you are experiencing.

Seeing your thoughts and feelings written in your own handwriting can have a very powerful therapeutic effect. In the following exercise, you can practise writing the steps down. This is a bit like a fill-in-the-blanks exercise because, the only thing that will change each time you write the steps down is the feeling, attitude, thought or emotion with which you are dealing. Do not write on the book instead, copy the steps on to a blank sheet of paper, leaving a space to write in your thoughts or feelings. When you are more familiar with exactly how to use the steps, you will do this your own way.

Protect Your Privacy

The main reason for not writing this exercise on the book is to protect your privacy. Your thoughts and feelings are a very intimate and private matter and therefore, should be treated with prudence. The point is that you may not want anyone, other than the person you share with, to have access to your private thoughts and feelings. You will also be destroying what you have written when finished as part of the letting go process. Therefore, do not write your thoughts and feelings on this or any other book unless you want them to be published.

To begin the exercise, get a blank sheet of paper, copy the example as presented below then fill in the blanks. When you are finished the exercise, dispose of the paper. Don't forget, you will still have to share the thoughts and feelings you are dealing with once you have them written down. There are two examples below: one for dealing with a thought, the other for dealing with a feeling. You can change the wording to suit whatever it is you are dealing with.

Example One:

Name it (write): *I am thinking about _____. I now let go of this thought.*
Share it (say to self and other): *I am thinking about _____. I now let go of this thought.*
Replace it (write and say to self): *I am clear headed at all times.*

Example Two:

Name it (write): *I am feeling _____. I now let go of this feeling.*
Share it (say to self and other): *I am feeling _____. I now let go of this feeling.*
Replace it (write and say to self): *I am safe and secure at all times and under all conditions.*

When you are finished applying the steps in this way, do not leave what you have written lying around. Dispose of it. A very powerful and symbolic way of letting go of thoughts and feelings is to burn the paper when you are finished and watch it go up in smoke. Don't forget, you will still have to practise step two, which is to share.

Sometimes it's best to practise step two before you destroy what you have written.

***

Stick to the Script

As you become more familiar with using the steps, you will be able to apply them quickly and more effectively. You will become more specific about naming and sharing your thoughts and feelings and you will find it easier to develop replacement affirmations to use in step three. This all means that you will be able to feel the benefits of using the three steps immediately. For now though, stick to the script.

Not Affirmations

You will learn about affirmations in greater detail later on but this is what you need to know right now. First, you need to be aware of the powerful effect the words you say have on your well-being. Next, the words used in the practice of steps one and two involve using an acknowledgement then a response. They are not functioning as affirmations they are simply words put together in the form of an acknowledgement and response. The acknowledgement: "I am afraid of…" is immediately followed by a response: "I now let go of this fear of…". The only affirmations used in the three steps is in the application of step three. For example: *I am safe and secure at all times and under all conditions*. This is an affirmation and can actually be used and repeated at any time and as many times as you want.

Using Step Three Affirmations

You can use the affirmations in step three or indeed any affirmation as a standalone exercise. To do this simply repeat an affirmation three times, pausing between each repetition for two or three seconds. However, although this is a good habit to get into and has its benefits, without the first two steps it will take much longer for affirmations to take hold. The main reason for this is that for many people the old attitude and way of thinking is sometimes so firmly established that when you try to introduce a new idea, thought or feeling it will be resisted and quickly overcome by the old more established mindset. Therefore, the best and most efficient way to apply affirmations is to use them with the three steps that is, immediately after practicing steps one and two apply step three. This allows the affirmation to take hold faster because the old troublesome feeling, attitude, thought or emotion has been removed.

Best Together

In effect the three steps work best together. When you let go of troublesome feelings, attitudes, thoughts and emotions using the first two steps, this creates what is best described as a vacuum. This vacuum needs to be filled immediately, otherwise it will quickly attract and suck in even more troublesome thoughts and feelings.

Therefore, affirmations are used immediately in step three to fill the vacuum. This is why the affirmations take hold quickly and the main reason why the three steps work best together. When affirmations are used in this way, the desired benefit becomes established immediately because there is nothing to prevent this from happening.

Being Specific

If you want to deal effectively with troublesome thoughts and feelings, you will need to be as specific as possible in relation to what you are dealing with. Therefore, as mentioned earlier the words you use to describe what you are feeling and thinking are very important. One of the reasons people have difficulty dealing with fear is because they are not specific enough as to what they are afraid of.

A particular fear that comes up a lot is fear around flying. In trying to manage this fear, many people talk about the fear of flying. However when questioned and asked to be more specific about what they are actually afraid of, many acknowledge that it is not the fear of flying they are afraid of but a fear of dying in a plane crash.

This means that the real fear cannot be dealt with because it is never really addressed and so, it remains and continues to grow. If you are not specific enough about the thought or feeling you are dealing with, you will not be able to deal with it. The more specific you are, the more you will be able to manage your thoughts and feelings, whatever they are.

Simple Not Easy

Dealing with a fearful situation or dealing with a specific fear is simple but sometimes, it may not be easy. The most difficult part of step one can often be having to say to yourself, "I am afraid."

Once you get over this hurdle, the fear will start to ease. It is important to be aware that fear is a natural instinct and therefore, it is okay to be afraid. It is good practice to acknowledge to yourself that it is okay to be afraid but, it is not okay to have fear ruin your life. From now on, you know how to deal with fear, you have the answer: name it, share it and replace it. The three steps are absolutely essential when dealing with any kind of fear, rational or irrational or any other troublesome thoughts and feelings hanging around in your life.

No Time Like the Present

Remember, this is your quick guide to the three steps to managing thoughts and feelings. If you are persistent in your practice, the old troublesome thoughts and feelings will disappear and be replaced with peace of mind and contentment. There is more to this approach but this quick guide will show you how to start using the three core steps immediately, without having to go through detailed explanations at this time.

Up to now, you have learned how to use the steps on feelings, attitudes, thoughts and emotions you may want to let go of. If you are learning about this approach for the purpose of helping someone else, this is all the more reason to practise on yourself right now. The best way to learn how to use the steps is through practice. When you can practise them yourself then you will be able to pass them on to others.

It Depends on You

There are other things you need to be aware of as you take these first steps on your way to contentment and greater well-being. For example, your peace of mind and happiness are a matter of choice and that choice is ultimately yours. Leaving your misery behind depends only on you. In these pages, you will learn how to leave sadness and unhappiness behind but it is you who has to be willing to do what it takes. It is you who must walk the path to emotional and spiritual freedom. This approach will show you the way and if you are willing to do a little walking you will be richly rewarded.

Conflict

Something else you also need to be aware of as you set out on this part of your journey in life is that you may experience internal conflict. This can occur when you have to put yourself first; for some, it means that for the first time in your life, you will have to start putting your own well-being ahead of others. The main reason for this is that if you do not take care of your "self" you will not be able to take care of your loved ones.

This applies especially when dealing with your mental and spiritual health. It means you cannot help others at the expense of your own well-being. All that will happen is you will also become unwell and be unable to help yourself or anyone else. This can be an area of conflict because some people confuse self-care, self-preservation and self-love with self-centredness and selfishness.

Self-Love

The love of self here is nothing to do with vanity and egotistical attitudes and behaviours. It is all about being kind and compassionate towards yourself first and then towards others. The reality for human beings is that if you have no love for your own self, then you will be unable to love anyone else. You will be operating on well-intentioned but misguided emotions. This is not love but a passing fancy and usually ends in tears.

***

Sharing

Steps one and two are both heavily involved in the letting go process. Step two goes further than step one in that it requires you to share with someone, therefore you will need someone trustworthy to share with. Sharing is essential! Human beings are social beings and need one another to share with.

The good news is that once you have someone to share with, it can be done over a cup of coffee, on the telephone or by e-mail. In these days of COVID-19, most sharing has to be done with the help of technology but this too will pass and soon you will be able to enjoy afresh the close fellowship that is so important to human wellbeing. In the meantime, technology will have to suffice.

Over time, you will find that sharing with someone you trust is a very deep, powerful and spiritual experience. If you have difficulty finding someone you can trust and feel comfortable with, there are helplines available all over the world, where you can share anonymously until you find someone to share with. One of the great benefits of using a helpline is that you can share what is bothering you immediately and anonymously, with someone who cares. One such helpline is run by Samaritan volunteers and it is used in this publication to provide a guide and template you can use when sharing with any helpline in whatever country you live.

About Samaritans

Samaritans was set up initially to help in the prevention of suicide but since it's foundation it has broadened its befriending and listening activities to include sharing whatever is troubling you. It is operated by highly trained volunteers with whom you can share any of your thoughts and feelings. If you are in any way troubled by thoughts around suicide or self-harm, please do not hesitate to call and share with Samaritans or a similar helpline.

In Ireland, England, Scotland and Wales you can contact Samaritans on free phone 116 123 or by calling into one of their centres for a one-to-one sharing. At the time of writing, due to the COVID-19 pandemic, face-to-face contact is not possible with Samaritans but you can still phone, e-mail or write at any time of the day or night. This means that you can also contact them from anywhere in the world by letter or by e-mail. For example, if you are in a country where the Samaritans' telephone number does not work, you can share with them by e-mailing – **jo@samaritans.ie** or you can share by letter. I you decide to write a letter make sure to use the freepost line of the address and post to:

Freepost RSRB-KKBY-CYJK,
Chris
PO Box 9090
Stirling FK8 2SA

Many Other Helplines

There are also many other helplines like Samaritans around the world. For example, the Crisis Text Line: Canada and the USA – text 741741; UK – text 85258; Ireland – text 50808. These text lines are available 24/7. English speakers in the USA can ring the 1-800-273-8255. Spanish speakers ring 1-888628-9454. These numbers will soon be reduced to the three-digit number 988 if it hasn't already happened and will be available all across the USA. You will also find a comprehensive list of these helplines on **www.suicidestop.com**

Contact details for these helplines are made available a number of times throughout this book for your convenience. This is because it is essential that you have someone available to you immediately when you decide to name and share certain kinds of thoughts and feelings. This is especially important when dealing with issues around self-harm and suicide because, it is in the naming and then the sharing of these that the first signs of relief and freedom will be felt. Sharing with Samaritans or one of the other helplines is a fantastic way to practise step two and it is completely anonymous and confidential.

The Ideal Scenario

The ideal scenario would be to team up with someone who is willing to share with you and use the three steps as well. However, this may be difficult to bring about until COVID-19 is under control therefore, until you find such a person, do not hesitate to use a helpline to share. Sharing is essential to your well-being; this cannot be overstated.

Sharing is the engine of the three steps and it will carry you swiftly on your way to greater well-being if you continue to practice. The more you share, the more you will let go of troublesome thoughts and feelings and whatever else may be bothering you. This will allow peace and contentment to come into your life and become a permanent presence. Furthermore, the benefits of sharing will be multiplied if it is done in conjunction with the other two steps.

If you are sharing something without consciously acknowledging what you are actually doing, it will have some benefit for sure, but it will not sustain your peace of mind in the long run. To deal with troublesome thoughts and feelings permanently you will have to go a bit deeper. Therefore, if you want to get maximum benefit from sharing feelings, attitudes, thoughts and emotions on a helpline or with any other person you must first name it, before you share it, only then can you replace it.

Lighten the Load

When dealing with thoughts and feelings around self-harm and suicide, it is really essential to have someone to share with. Remember also that this applies to managing all troublesome thoughts and feelings. No matter what issue you are dealing with, sharing will lighten the load.

For instance, it may be that you have a relative or friend you are concerned about in relation to self-harm. Or maybe you have personal difficulties or worries that you need to share, if so, a helpline like Samaritans is a great first call, in particular, around the subjects of self-harm and suicide.

Whatever the issue, you can confidentially share whatever is troubling you with Samaritans. Don't forget, as mentioned earlier, the phone lines and e-mail responses are managed by highly trained volunteers and your conversations and communications are completely confidential. They are also free and require no obligation other than to use them when you need them.

About Self-Harm

Dealing with troublesome thoughts and feelings such as fear, anxiety, stress and loneliness will be common to most people at some time throughout their lives. Thoughts and feelings around self-harm and suicide are particularly troublesome for all and for many they are never too far away from their consciousness.

In these days of information overload, once you reach the age of reason, you will be constantly reminded of self-harm and suicide. This information comes to you via TV, social media, radio, newspapers and other information media. It is virtually impossible to avoid therefore it's best to know how to deal with it.

There are few people who will not have been impacted, in some way, by self-harm and suicide. Some people manage these thoughts and feelings better than others. The three steps offer a simple way to manage thoughts and feelings around self-harm and suicide that actually works. Freedom from this kind of troublesome thinking is life changing.

Dealing with Troublesome Thoughts around Self-Harm Quickly

As mentioned, trying to avoid issues around self-harm is very difficult, if not impossible therefore, you will need to be able to deal with them. If you are troubled right now around the matter of self-harm in the form of suicidal thinking apply the three steps as follows:

1. **Name it** (say to self): *I am thinking about suicide. I now let go of this thought.*
2. **Share it** (say to self and other): *I am thinking about suicide. I now let go of this thought.*
3. **Replace it** (say to self and or write): *I am safe and secure at all times.*

Repeat affirmations in step three slowly at least three times, remembering to pause for a few seconds between repetitions.

Thoughts and Feelings need to be Managed

As you grow and develop as a human being, sooner or later, you will discover that how you feel and how you think are central to everything you do as a human being. Therefore, thoughts and feelings need to be managed, no matter who you are, what you are, how much property you own, how successful you think you are or, how much money you have in the bank or under your bed.

If you are feeling depressed, anxious, stressed out, fearful, lonely, isolated, suicidal and or miserable, then your life is a living hell. These very troublesome thoughts and feelings need to be managed. The good news for you is that you now have the tools to deal with all your troublesome thoughts and feelings. The quick guide is to get you to start doing this immediately.

Quickly Mastered

The three steps will take just a few minutes to commit to memory and as you can see, can be applied in seconds. They can be applied to any troublesome thoughts or feelings, whenever or wherever they occur. Practise them every chance you get until they are a spontaneous response to any emotional disturbances. Through daily and even hourly practice, they will be quickly mastered and your life will be transformed.

There will be times when you will need to apply the steps often throughout your day but, that depends on how deep-rooted and troublesome your thoughts and feelings are. With practice, you will gain control and your life will be transformed beyond all your expectations.

CHAPTER THREE

Mastery

In this chapter you will be introduced to the idea of mastering your feelings, attitudes, thoughts and emotions. You will be presented with four principles that you will find particularly useful as you continue your journey in life. They can be used on any skill you are trying to perfect.

There is a book and also a film called *The Legend of Bagger Vance* (1995) by Steven Pressfield, in which four principles are presented as a means to achieving mastery. These four principles are presented in relation to the game of golf but they can actually be applied to any activity you are trying to master.

They are introduced at this point to let you know that you can master any discipline you set your mind to. If you apply these principles to this approach to achieving contentment and greater well-being, you will basically become the master of your own fate.

There is a great deal of personal satisfaction associated with mastering a particular skill but even more so in mastering your own thoughts and feelings.

Apply in Anything You are Trying to Achieve

The four principles of mastery are simply suggestions and if applied correctly, will help make mastering your thoughts and feelings as painless as possible. They can literally be applied to whatever it is you are trying to master: the three steps, baking a cake, walking, all the other suggestions in this book, the list goes on.

In relation to this approach to well-being, all the suggestions in this book are simple to apply and with a little bit of persistence can be mastered quickly. Just remember, when you first start to practise anything new, it is going to feel strange and awkward until you familiarise yourself with it. This approach is no different but it is simpler than most of the things that you will have to learn in life.

The Four Principles:

Learn about It
Practice It
Love it
Let go

Learn About It

To learn about it you will need knowledge about what it is you are trying to master. Learning about anything will involve some kind of investigation or study. One of the ways to do this is to read about it. Since you are reading this book, you are already acquiring knowledge on how to master your thoughts and feelings. This means you are already on the way to mastery. To keep your progress going you will need to continue to read and learn as much as you can about the skill you are trying to master.

Remember the same principles apply to anything you might want to master. For example if you are trying to master mindfulness meditation first learn about it. Read about it and discover as much as you can about it. Find someone who meditates and ask them to show you how it's done. See if there are any meditation groups in your area. By the way, you will find a wealth of information and articles on mindfulness and meditation on the internet.

These are just a few ways you can acquire knowledge and learn about what it is you wish to master. The point is, whatever you are trying to master, you will need to have knowledge about it and to acquire this you will need to learn about it.

Practice It

Next you will need to practice it. If you really want to manage your thoughts and feelings and be at your best in whatever it is that you do, practice is essential. More specifically, correct practice is essential. To do this you will need to check and recheck your routine to ensure you are practising correctly. No amount of practising something wrong will make it right.

Let's say you want to check if you are practicing the steps correctly one way to do this is to measure and monitor how you are feeling. This will mean that you will have to measure and monitor how you are feeling and thinking over a number of days, weeks or months. You will discover a very simple way to measure and monitor your progress in the next chapter.

How Well are you Practising?

Generally, changes in your behaviour are a good indicator of how well you are practising. You can get a good idea of how well you are doing by asking yourself one simple question. If for example you are trying to change a particular behaviour ask yourself, has my behaviour changed? If it hasn't, you will need to look at the way you are practising and make the necessary changes.

Love It

If you do not love doing whatever it is that you are trying to do then you will never master it. You will have to stop doing it altogether or change your attitude towards it. For example, if you do not love or grow to love the practice of managing your thoughts and feelings it is very unlikely that you will master it. You will quickly give up. Therefore this attitude would have to change. If you find yourself with this attitude you can use the three steps to change it as follows:

Name it (to self): *I don't want to manage my thoughts and feelings. I now let go of this attitude.*
Share it (self and other): *I don't want to manage my thoughts and feelings. I now let go of this attitude.*
Replace it (say): *I love being able to manage my thoughts and feelings. Repeat x 3! Pause for a couple of seconds between repetitions.*

Reminder! When using affirmations as in step three it is always good practice to repeat them a number of times. It is also very important to pause for a few seconds between repetitions to let the affirmation sink in. This is because more often than not you will be affirming the opposite to what you may feel and think. The pause gives the mind time to become aware that a different thought or idea has been introduced but not enough time to reject it.

When you first start to use the steps or indeed anything you are not familiar with, it will feel awkward and uncomfortable. This will change with practice and in particular when practising the steps, you will quickly come to love what you are doing as you begin to feel the effects. Regular practice of the three steps will change how you feel and think and you will quickly grow to love replacing troublesome feelings, attitudes, thoughts and emotions unconditionally.

Let Go

Letting go here means getting out of your own way. It involves coming to a realisation that there are faculties and talents available to you that, up to now, you were not aware of. You will get some understanding of letting go, in the context of mastery, if you liken it to being inspired. You move beyond the confines of thoughts and feelings and into the world of "spirituality".

In this condition, nothing can stop you from achieving your goal. Just like the athlete or musician who, having done their practice, learned about their discipline, love what they do they can then move on to another level of being. On this level they are able to let go completely because feelings, attitudes, thoughts and emotions are excluded.

In this state the athlete is ready to perform at their best and the musician is able to produce magical musical improvisations. This level of being is easily achievable if you are willing to follow the simple guidelines set out here. You can move into a world that, up to this time in your life, you could only have imagined.

How Long Does It Take?

The question as to how long it takes to become a master often arises. Being aware of and practising these four principles will quickly bring you to a level of mastery in relation to this approach to happiness and well-being. The amazing thing is that the mastery of the approach presented in these pages can be achieved in an instant. In fact, mastery of anything can be achieved instantly. It just requires being open-minded, honest and willing to do whatever it takes to change for the better, without question. This means letting nothing deter you from your goal. The more willing you are the more you will be amazed at the transformation and how quickly it takes place.

CHAPTER FOUR

Measuring and Monitoring

At this stage, you have at least started to practise the steps. If not, this is the time to begin. Once you know what you have to do, the three steps can be applied in seconds. Measuring and monitoring is no different in that, it too takes only seconds to carry out – when you know how.

Just like doing anything that you are not familiar with, measuring and monitoring will seem strange at first. However, once you have practised it a few times, it will quickly become second nature to you. This exercise will also give you the benefit of seeing a snapshot of your progress in relation to your thoughts and feelings generally.

There is a subtle difference between measuring and monitoring. When you are measuring your progress, you will be able to see how you are doing in the present moment. On the other hand, when you are monitoring your progress, you will be observing your progress over a period of time for example a week or a month.

How You Feel Now

To begin, you will need some way of measuring how you are feeling and thinking that allows you to quickly establish your progress as to your level of peace and happiness at any given time. Beyond that measuring your progress a number of times over a period of time (for example: a day, a week, month or even a year) will allow you to monitor your progress over that period of time. This is an essential exercise as it will enable you to establish how well you are doing by checking your progress or lack of it.

Write It Down

Although measuring your thoughts and feelings is basically a simple mental exercise that you can do anytime or anywhere, you will also need to keep a record of how you are doing over a period of time. This will mean you have to write down how you feel and keep a record of it. The good news is that measuring and monitoring are both simple and easy to do but as mentioned earlier when you do it for the first time, it will feel strange.

You will first need to learn how to measure your feelings, attitudes, thoughts and emotions. The easiest way to do this is on a simple numerical scale, where you can see, at a glance, how you are doing.

Before you continue through the rest of this chapter keep in mind that some people will already be familiar with these kinds of scales but some will not. This is why a very brief introduction to these measuring scales is set out in the next paragraphs. If you are already familiar with them you will know how simple they are to use.

Measuring Scales

There are a number of scales that can be adapted for use in measuring your feelings, attitude, thoughts and emotions. The visual analogue scale (VAS) attributed to the work of Hayes and Patterson in the early 1920s is one scale that can be used. There is also the numerical rating scale (NRS) which appears to have been derived from the VAS. These scales are used extensively to measure the level of physical pain, psychological discomfort and also the level of satisfaction being experienced. A combination of these scales will provide the simplest and most effective option to measure thoughts and feelings. This scale is simple to use and gives an accurate result quickly, if utilised properly.

Remember, this is an exercise in self-monitoring. It is therefore essential that you are as sincere and honest with yourself as you can possibly be when using this scale. This will ensure that you can get an accurate account as to how you are doing.

The Scale

The scale used here is made up of a set of numbers ranging from 0 to 10, set out in a straight line across a page with two extreme positions at each end. To measure physical pain, the scale would look something like:

1	2	3	4	5	6	7	8	9	10

no pain   extreme pain

How the Scale Works

As mentioned earlier you may already be familiar with how this type of scale works, as it is often used by the medical profession to measure physical pain. For instance, if you are in physical pain, a medical practitioner may ask you to pick a number between one and ten that best describes the level of pain you are experiencing, where 0 represents no pain and 10 extreme pain. This number is then recorded and now, there is a record of the level of physical pain you may be suffering.

Measuring Feelings, Attitude, Thoughts and Emotions

The same type of scale can be used to measure your feelings, attitude, thoughts and emotions (FATE). To begin measuring your FATE it is a good idea to copy the following scales on to a blank sheet of paper as they are set out here:

Measuring Feelings

1	2	3	4	5	6	7	8	9	10

extremely
sad

extremely
happy

Measuring Attitude

1	2	3	4	5	6	7	8	9	10

extremely
tolerant

extremely
intolerant

Measuring Thoughts

1	2	3	4	5	6	7	8	9	10

insignificant
thinking

extreme
thinking

Measuring Emotions

1	2	3	4	5	6	7	8	9	10

extreme calm

panic

Next mark or circle the number that best represents the intensity of the feeling, attitude, thought or emotion you are experiencing on the scale. For example, if you are measuring how happy you are and you circle 2 on the feelings scale, it means you are extremely sad or unhappy; if you circle 8, you are extremely happy. When you are actually doing this exercise do not over think it. Do it quickly but as honestly and sincerely as you can.

You will become more accurate with practice.

Extremes

In the example dealing with physical pain, there is only one extreme that is extreme pain. Obviously in this example you will want to have no pain. In the four examples dealing with feelings, attitudes, thoughts and emotions, you have two extremes. In these examples you will not want to be in any of the extremes. Instead, you will be trying to achieve a balance, somewhere in the middle, between the two extremes.

Extremes of any kind of feeling, attitude, thought or emotion in the main do not last. If they do, it is an indication that something is out of balance. Therefore, you will want to take some kind of action to get back to a position of balance which is somewhere in the middle of the scale.

In the material world everything is continually changing and adapting to its environment. Because of their connection with the material world feelings, attitudes, thoughts and emotions are also constantly changing. These kinds of changes can be identified as highs or lows on the scales and are indicators of your overall well-being. Extreme highs and extreme lows of any kind cannot be sustained for long periods of time without unhealthy consequences.

Moderation

When you are measuring thoughts and feelings using these scales, you will be seeking the middle ground or moderation; this is the balance. When you are in balance, the numbers on the scale will be vibrating within a range of 4 and 7. Every now and then, you may hit an 8 or a 9 at one end of the scale or drop to a 2 or a 3 at the other end. These extreme variations are rare but can occur for example, if you win a lottery your happiness may hit a 9 briefly. On the other hand, in times of sudden grief or sorrow, your level of sadness may drop to 2 or even 1. These extreme variations are perfectly natural and generally will pass quickly but staying in any of the extremes for long periods of time is not healthy and you will, sooner or later, have to get back into balance.

Handling Extremes

If you find yourself remaining in any of these extremes for longer than you want, try to practise the steps more vigilantly, paying particular attention to your sharing. In addition, as you go through the rest of this book, you will find the chapter on mindfulness and awareness (see Chapter 14) very helpful for preventing episodes of extremes and will also facilitate a return to balance quickly.

When you use this type of scale to measure how you are feeling, you will always be seeking the balance of moderation. One of the keys to peace of mind and contentment is the practice of moderation. Beyond that, the final three chapters will explain how to prevent other extremes coming into your life and ensure your lasting peace of mind and mental fitness.

The Importance of Measuring

Please do not let the simplicity of doing this measuring exercise prevent you from doing it. It is the action of doing and taking responsibility for your own wellbeing that generates the energy you need to change how you are feeling and thinking. Without action, nothing happens. Remember, what you are doing is for you, not for anyone else. Others may benefit from your wellbeing but for now, you have got to do this for yourself.

Measuring your feelings, attitudes, thoughts and emotions is ultimately as simple as picking a number between 0 and 10 and making a note of it. The reason for spending time explaining how to create and use this scale is to make sure you know what you are doing and you know the importance of doing it right. The difficulty with this exercise and all the exercises in this book is not in knowing what you have to do but in actually doing them.

One of Two

Once you have become familiar with measuring your progress you will then be able to begin monitoring how you are doing. This will allow you to keep track of your progress over a period of time (for example: days, weeks or even years). After practising the three steps over a sustained period of time and measuring and noting your progress, you will start to see a trend or a movement away from extreme feelings to more moderate fluctuations of your thoughts and feelings in general. This is actually the reason for monitoring your progress and why you should record how you are feeling. Measuring your progress is the first part of a two-part process.

Monitoring Your Progress

The second part of the process is monitoring. These two exercises are carried out together. Monitoring your progress will tell you how well you are doing over a period of time (a day, week or year). Measuring, on the other hand, will tell you how you are at a particular point in time.

To monitor your progress, you must first measure your FATE then record the measurement. Let's say that you want to monitor your feelings of stress over a period of a week. First measure your stress levels three times a day in the morning, in the middle of your day and last thing at night using the scale as follows:

Mark and Record

Measuring Stress

1	2	3	4	5	6	7	8	9	10

no stress   **extreme stress**

On the scale, pick a number between 0 and 10 that best describes your stress levels. Mark this number on the scale. This will give you a visual as to where you are at in relation to how you are feeling. Record this number in a notebook or handwritten diary. Do this exercise each morning, afternoon and night for one week and at the end of the week, check to see how the figures look. Make sure you also record the date and time that you take the measurement each day.

Date: Monday 01 Jan 2021
Morning: 4
Afternoon: 3 Night: 6

In some diaries, along with the date, times will also be printed. In this case all you will have to do is write in the number beside the time.

No Analysis

Try not to over think or dwell too much on what you are doing. If you are practising the steps and this exercise correctly, the numbers will be changing as the days go by. Remaining at 2 or 9 for long periods of time, for example: a day, a week or more indicate the need to change something. Moving between 4 and 7 with the occasional jump to 8 or even 9 is the balance you will be looking for. Remember, extremes of anything are to be avoided. Again try not to over think or analyse what you are doing.

Even if you have to guess at how you feel, this is better than over thinking it. It should take no more than a few seconds to pick a number and write it down. If it takes longer than three or four seconds to do this, you are over thinking it.

You will get better at this exercise the more you do it. Be patient with yourself. You will become familiar with this exercise very quickly if you practise it a few times a day. Once you are familiar with it you will be able to apply it in seconds.

The Diary

It's a very good idea to get your hands on a paper diary that also has the time (usually on the hour) printed on it for the purpose of measuring and monitoring your progress. You can also use it for recording any other important information or ideas you come across as you continue your journey. For example, it can be used for drawing your scales and for writing your own affirmations.

Having a handwritten diary or notebook to record important information may seem like an ancient practice in these days of smart phones and other technology. However, it is the best way to do these exercises. The act of writing without the aid of an electronic device is very therapeutic in itself. This is especially true when you are writing in relation to thoughts and feelings. It is why handwriting is recommended for these exercises.

Technology is a wonderful tool to have at your disposal but not for these exercises. Therefore, as you will be physically writing and recording numbers, a paper diary is best suited for this purpose. Of course you can use any book you choose but it will need to be small enough for you to carry it with you at all times.

About Technology and this Exercise

Do not use a computer or smart phone for this exercise. There is nothing wrong with technology; it is just that smart phones and computers are often closely connected with work life and many other things that can cause stress, anxiety, worry and fear. For these reasons, electronic instruments are best avoided. So again, use a diary or notebook to hand write your numbers.

Likewise, it will be more beneficial for you to avoid using a computer to make copies of the scale. Draw the scales by hand. This action alone is hugely beneficial and empowering but you will only know this when you do it.

Time for Analysis

If you are monitoring and recording how you feel three times a day, morning, afternoon and night. At the end of the week, write the numbers down in three columns under the headings, morning, afternoon and evening. Next check to see how you are doing. For example, check if the numbers change from morning to morning. Do they change throughout the day? Do the numbers differ from morning to afternoon or night? Are the numbers consistently too high or low? Remember, the balance that you are seeking is to have the numbers move up and down somewhere between 4 and 7 generally, with the occasional bounce to an 8 or 9, or drop to 1 or 2. Remember, if the numbers are too high or too low consistently throughout the week, you will need to focus the steps on reducing your stress levels.

Naming and sharing your anxieties and other stressors will help reduce your stress levels and remember, the chapter on simple meditation techniques (see Chapter 14) will also help to reduce your stress levels.

Persistence Brings Confidence

Doing these exercises a number of times each day is a great way to get familiar with it. Once you have learned how to use the measuring and monitoring tools, it takes just seconds to apply them. When using them to measure how you are doing over a day, it is good practice to measure about three times during the day at regular intervals. Also, make sure to note the times that you do the exercise. Daily practice will help you become more confident in your life overall.

The purpose of this chapter is to introduce you to measuring how you feel and then monitoring your progress, so that you can take remedial action if you need to do so. Being involved in your own development and well-being in this way is hugely therapeutic and empowering in itself.

CHAPTER FIVE

What Now?

So far, you have been introduced to the three core steps of this approach and how to use them. You have discovered how to master new skills and also learned how to measure and monitor your FATE.

In this chapter, you will be introduced to a way of establishing where you are and where you are going. You will see your progress as it might appear on a graph, so that you can get some insight into where you are and how you are doing. In this chapter too, you will be introduced to the idea of doing an emotional inventory, before going on to complete it in the following chapter.

Where are You?

Being able to get some sense of where you are and where you are going will make all your journeys in life more manageable and less stressful. This is especially true when you take the first steps in managing your thoughts and feelings. Because if you don't know where you are or where you are going you will never get anywhere. This is why the exercises and the rest of these discussions are so important they will help you establish where you are, find your way if you get lost and familiarise you with what to expect as your journey continues.

Take it Easy

As you become more familiar with the exercises through practice, you will quickly begin to see how simple the whole process is. On the other hand you will also begin to understand that what you are doing and why, may take a bit longer. There is quite a bit of material to get your head around in this book but you do not have to go through everything at once. The only thing you may need to do immediately is to memorise and practise the three core steps then work your way through the rest at your own pace.

Your journey to greater well-being will take you through many stages. Some of these will be more obvious than others but remember, each exercise is simple and can be practised in seconds. They are designed to fit seamlessly into your lifestyle, no matter how busy you are. The longer meditations will require a little more time to learn and practise but it is entirely up to you how much of this you want to do.

A Bit Unsure

The chances are right now you are still a bit unsure about where you are on your journey. It is quite possible that one minute, you feel like you are soaring effortlessly across the sky and next, you feel like you are wearing lead boots. This is not unusual and has often been described as feeling like a yo-yo. Actually, going up and down like a yo-yo is a good description.

In fact, if you were to take the data or the numbers you have recorded during the measuring and monitoring exercise and put them in a graph, that is exactly what your progress would look like: going up and down like a yo-yo. If this approach is being applied correctly, this up and down movement will be within a band that is continually progressing.

The Graph

The graph is for illustration purposes only but it does give a number of important insights. For instance it will give you a visual of what your progress might look like. It lets you see where you might be on your journey towards well-being. It shows your destination as a continuous progression. It also illustrates that progress rarely if ever evolves in a straight line.

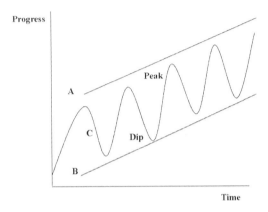

This is what your progress might look like on a graph (JPF2nd)

For the purpose of this book, progress is represented as a continuous curved line C, which is going up and down within a band A and B. This band is sloping upwards towards greater well-being representing continuous progress.

In any kind of personal development work and especially in relation to thoughts and feelings, progress is never a straight line. Paradoxically you will always be making progress even though sometimes it may feel like you are going backwards. During these times, you need to know what is happening. So, if you feel like you are going backwards or getting worse, all that is happening is that you are moving towards the dip in the curved line C on the graph.

If you are practising the three steps, you will only go as far as the dip before you begin to go back up towards the peak in the curved line C. This up and down movement indicates your emotional state and therefore the peaks and dips are temporary. Your goal will always be working towards flattening this curved line. Although this line is never actually flattened.

Always Improving

What you need to be aware of, right now, is that once you start applying the steps and the other suggestions, you will always be improving.

Between the lines in the graph progress is illustrated, not by a straight line but, as was mentioned earlier, one that is going up and down inside the band A and B. Within that band, progress will always be in a state of fluctuation that is, it will be going up and going down peaking and dipping. These emotional fluctuations are to be expected but once you keep practising the steps, you will feel more and more at ease with yourself.

If this ease were to be illustrated on the graph, it would be seen as a flattening of the curve line C although, it will never be completely flat. There will always be some emotional movement in C but this will, eventually, become more like hills and valleys, rather than peaks and dips and more in line with a balanced emotional state.

Tangible and Intangible

The graph gives you something tangible to work with, bearing in mind that when you are managing thoughts and feelings, you are dealing with the intangible. This means that you cannot see, hear, taste, smell or touch them physically but, you know they are there. This is one of the reasons why the graph is so important and useful, it allows you to see the intangible.

By the way, although the graph is only intended for illustration purposes, you can actually enter the numbers you have recorded when you did your measuring and monitoring exercise. This is very much optional but if you are so inclined, you might like to do that. When you are managing thoughts and feeling, you will always be trying to make progress. Remember, whatever helps to keep you on track is worth doing over and over. You can never overdose on what is good for you.

One other thing to be aware of is that no one does this, or anything else for that matter, perfectly. The best that you can hope for is to make progress in anything you do.

Willingness and Open-mindedness

Willingness and open-mindedness go hand in hand. Developing these qualities is essential to your continued success in managing thoughts and feelings and overall development. The simplest way to begin developing these qualities is through the use of affirmations. If you have been practising the steps, you have already been practising affirmations in step three.

To use affirmations to help you cultivate open-mindedness and willingness, say and repeat the following affirmations as often as you like, remember to pause for a couple of seconds between each repetition:

I am willing to change
I am willing to try
I am willing to be open-minded

If you are on your own, it is a good practice to say affirmations out loud. If you are in company, you can say them in your mind. Repeat these affirmations until willingness to change and open-mindedness are a way of life for you. Again, one way to use an affirmation is to say it, wait a few seconds, then say it again. To complete the above exercise repeat for each affirmation. It is also a good practice to write affirmations down. You can use your notebook for this purpose. Of course as mentioned earlier the best way to use affirmations is with the three steps.

Emotional Baggage

Now that you have started out on this journey towards greater well-being you need to know how to identify and then let go of deep-rooted, emotional baggage. This kind of emotional baggage may include the likes of resentments, guilt, shame, blame, jealousy and past hurts that are carried around. These will sabotage your progress and if you do not deal with them, they will deal with you.

Everyone has emotional baggage, tons of it. Sometimes it is carried around like a prized possession. You may even think no one knows it's there but you can be sure that there are those who know it's there. The truth is, although emotional baggage may not be seen by everyone there are people in your life who know it's there. Emotional baggage is always tightly packed and waits patiently until somebody annoys you or rubs you up the wrong way that's when it shows up for all to see. Holding on to emotional baggage is absolutely useless and detrimental to your progress.

Emotional Inventory

The best and simplest way to let go of your emotional baggage is to do an emotional inventory. You will discover how to do this type of inventory in the next chapter. When it is completed, it will be a giant step on your journey. It involves doing an inventory of all your feelings, attitudes, thoughts and emotions (FATE). The main purpose of doing this exercise is to identify all, or as much as possible, the emotional baggage you need to let go and replace. As with all the other exercises in this book it is simple to do but powerful.

Self-Honesty

Because doing an emotional inventory is a self-assessment exercise the only way you can benefit from it is by being honest with yourself. When doing the exercise remember it is for your eyes only so you can be as explicit as you like. The only thing that other people will see are the changes for the better taking place in you. Doing an inventory of your feelings, attitudes, thoughts and emotions is an exercise in emotional stocktaking. It is very revealing and really worth taking a few minutes to complete. Once it is completed, you will be able to see at a glance, what you need to let go of immediately and it will keep you up to date as to where you are at in relation to your overall well-being.

Stocktaking?

Stocktaking itself is an accounting term, mainly used in business to account for all the goods the business is trading in and all other assets and liabilities. It is a very practical exercise and involves naming, recording and establishing the condition of all items of stock used in the business. You can see how important this activity is to a business. Likewise, your emotional stock is essential for your well-being and happiness. Your feelings, attitudes, thoughts and emotions are all part of your emotional stock and they can be either assets or liabilities.

Keep It Simple

When doing this exercise for the first time, keep it very simple and again, do not over think it. You will do this exercise many times in your life, so if you miss something, you will get it next time around. Therefore, always try to keep it simple and do the best you can.

It is never necessary to go looking for troublesome thoughts and feelings during this or any of the other exercises, they will find you. You do not need to go analysing your childhood or rooting around in your past for reasons why you may be feeling the way you feel today.

Your future is not in your past. Just account for the thoughts and feelings that come to mind immediately. In doing this, any other thoughts and feelings that need to be dealt with will surface when you are ready to deal with them. For now, keep it simple and deal with the obvious ones.

Something else that you need to be aware of as you go on. Thoughts and feelings come and then they go, if you let them, therefore, just spend a few minutes at a time on this exercise, then leave it for another time. Of course, you can do it as often as you wish, every day if you like.

Chapter Six

Emotional Stocktaking

In this chapter, you will learn how to carry out an emotional stocktaking inventory. This is a very simple exercise. It would be a good idea to practise it immediately after you read through this chapter. When dealing with troublesome thoughts and feelings the answers are always simple. One way to keep things simple for your self is to practise the exercises after you read through them. This will also help you memorise the exercises and decide what you need to work on most at this time.

If you are an experienced traveller of any kind, you will know that every journey you make begins with one step then another. The journey towards happiness and peace of mind is no different and like any journey, if you are not familiar with the road ahead it can feel uncomfortable and sometimes even fearful.

On the other hand if you have a decent mode of transport and willing to follow your guide you will be able to avoid many of the bumps on the road and have a very pleasant journey. These exercises are your transport and your guide.

The Journey is Home

The emotional stocktaking exercise is just another part of your mode of transport, designed to help make the journey as painless as possible. As you go forward, keep in mind that you are on what is the greatest undertaking of your life, that is your journey towards lasting peace and contentment. If you apply the exercises sincerely, you will speed up the process and you will feel the benefits.

To begin using this exercise start by making an emotional stocktaking table. This simply means making a list of your emotional assets and your emotional liabilities. The goal of this exercise is to establish what your assets and liabilities are, before letting them go and then, replacing them.

Assets and Liabilities

Find some place private where you can be alone. Take a blank sheet of paper and a writing pen. Divide the paper into two halves by drawing a straight line down the middle of the page. Write the words *Emotional Assets* as a heading on the top of the left-hand side of the page. Write the words Emotional Liabilities as a heading on the right-hand side of the page. Draw a line across the page underlining the two headings.

Next, make a list of all the emotional assets and liabilities you think you have under the appropriate heading. An example of an emotional asset would be, 'I am loving'. An example of an emotional liability would be, 'I hate my myself'. When you have completed these lists, you have now completed an inventory. It's that simple!

It is best to keep your emotional inventories short and manageable but you can do this exercise as often as you like. A simple emotional inventory might look something like the following table:

Emotional Stocktaking Table

Emotional Assets	Emotional Liabilities
I am loving	I hate my job
I am forgiving	I am resentful
I am patient	I am intolerant
I am kind	I am inconsiderate

Now Let Them All Go

Once you have listed and accounted for all your emotional assets and liabilities, you will have identified and named them. Your feelings, attitudes, thoughts and emotions, troublesome or otherwise are now out in the open and written down in front of you. This means you can now let them all go. This will involve destroying the paper on which they are written. Before going on to that, you may be wondering why you need to let go of them all.

Why Let Them All Go

It will probably be obvious to you why you will need to let go of emotional liabilities. However, just in case it is not obvious, it is because your liabilities will be hurting you and causing you pain. What will not be as obvious is the reason for letting go of your emotional assets. So the question is often asked, why do you need to let go of your emotional assets? Surely, it makes sense to hold on to these after all, they are assets. The answer in this case is no everything must go.

Everything Must Go

To get the full benefit of this exercise, everything in the inventory must go, this includes liabilities, assets and old ideas. It's important for you to grasp the need to do this because you do not want anything hanging around that's going to prevent or slow down your progress. Along with giving you a visual of where you are emotionally, doing this exercise will clear your mind. It will allow you to start your life afresh every time you do it and has the effect of setting everything in your life to zero. This effect cannot be achieved until your mind is emptied completely.

A Tall Order

For some, this will take a lot of getting used to and will be resisted by your mind. It will not want you managing and interfering with its stock. However, perseverance and simplicity will force your mind into submission. Your mind will not want or like simplicity and once you have done this inventory a few times, it will get bored and no longer resist.

It is good practice to do this exercise a number of times to get familiar with it. When you begin, practise it often and once you are familiar with it, use it to make sure there are no skeletons left behind in your mental cupboards. Doing this exercise may appear like a tall order but it will be worth it. As time goes by, you will be able to use this inventory as a means to clear out mental clutter whenever you feel the need. For example you can do it weekly, monthly, yearly whenever you want to clear your mind.

Once the emotional stocktaking exercise is completed you can use your list of emotional assets and liabilities as part of the practice of the three steps. In fact when you look closely at what is happening when you do this exercise you can see that it is actually a more indebt way of practising step one. In this case it facilitates the acknowledgement, identification and the naming of thoughts and feelings. To multiply the benefit of doing the emotional stocktaking share your experience.

***

Sharing Your Experience

Sharing after you have completed the emotional stocktaking exercise is a more in-depth application of step two. It is at the heart of every human experience and if practised often enough, over time it will create an unbreakable bond between the sharer and the listener. Sharing is the act of telling another human being your thoughts and your feelings for the purpose of letting them go.

As always, caution and prudence are advised when sharing. You may want or even need the assistance of a professional for some of your sharing. If so, there are all kinds of help available for this purpose. This includes therapists, counsellors, psychotherapists, psychologists, life coaches and helplines. If you have specific needs in any area, you will want to seek out the most suitable person to share with.

Someone to Share With

Sharing and having someone to share with is absolutely essential therefore the contact details for Samaritans and other groups are set out here again for your convenience. To call Samaritans in Ireland, England, Scotland, Wales dial 116 123. You can also e-mail **jo@samaritans.ie** from anywhere in the world or you can write to them at their postal address, you will find it in Chapter 2. Samaritans are just one of the many helplines around the world providing this service. You can find out more about them on their website at www.samaratans.org. If you are based in Canada or the US, you can share by texting the Crisis Text Line 741741. The Crisis Text Line is also available in the UK – text 85258. In Ireland, text 086 1800 280. You will find a comprehensive list of helplines at www.suicidestop.com

Using a Therapist to Share

If you decide to use a therapist for the purpose of sharing, you may have to attend a session or two to see if there is a good fit between you and the therapist. They will need to have certain qualities such as kindness, compassion and trustworthiness. If you feel these characteristics are not present, then this is not the right therapist for you. Remember, this is all about you and your well-being, not the therapist and you must feel comfortable with the person you are going to share and confide in.

Again, remember Samaritans are always available to listen at the other end of a phone line. They are also available online and will always respect your privacy. You can also remain anonymous when using Samaritans or other helplines. So, if you need someone immediately, you can always use their helpline or the other helplines mentioned, to share personal thoughts and feelings. Sharing in this way can sometimes be the best therapy.

Careful Who You Share With

If you wish to share with someone who you are already close to, make sure they possess the three qualities mentioned above: kindness, compassion and trustworthiness. Ask them a few questions without making it too obvious that you are actually interviewing them. For example, ask what they think about people sharing feelings with each other. Open a conversation about the approach in this book. Ask their opinion about it. Ask if they would be willing to share thoughts and feelings! Their response will be an indicator as to whether this person is suitable and a good fit for you or not.

It may take a bit of time to find someone in this way. Until you do remember you always have the helplines, in fact you could use both. Be patient! It is really important to know someone really well before you share anything too deep with them. Choose wisely!

The Suitability Test

Ask yourself the following questions about them. Is this person kind? Is this person compassionate? Is this person trustworthy? If the answer is yes to these three questions, this person will more than likely be a good fit for you.

Further questions you can ask yourself about the person as proof of their suitability. Do they gossip? Do they talk or say nasty things to you about others? If the answer is yes to these questions, they will surely talk about you to someone else. If you know the person, you will already know the answers to these questions but you may have never thought about them in relation to these kinds of questions. You must choose wisely!

***

Thoughts and Feelings Come and then they Go

You may not be aware that thoughts and feelings come and then they go if you let them! Unfortunately, some people hold on to some thoughts and feelings until they become emotional liabilities. Now that you are aware of this you will no longer hold on to these liabilities and you will be able to let them go. Once you have completed an emotional stocktaking exercise and shared you will be well on the way.

You will have identified and cleared most of the emotional baggage that has been making your life difficult and at times miserable. The application of emotional stocktaking is a very thorough way to practise step one, it helps to uncover thoughts and feelings, along with other old ideas that need to be dealt with. After they are shared, they will be gone and will remain gone once they are replaced.

Physical, Mental and Spiritual Pain

If you hold on to troublesome feelings, attitudes, thoughts and emotions, sooner or later they will cause physical, mental and spiritual pain. When this pain gets bad enough, it will have to be treated in some way. This will involve some form of medication or some kind of therapy. The reality of this is that, unless you want to end up taking some kind of prescribed medication or be dependent on other chemicals, you will have to practise some form of therapeutic remedy. The approach to greater well-being presented in this book is one such remedy. It can also be used alongside any other form of remedy you may be using.

You cannot stop thoughts and feelings coming into your life, they come and they go. They will flow into your life and they will flow out again but you have to let them. For most people this is what happens unfortunately some will hold on to thoughts and feelings especially the troublesome ones until they hurt really bad. This can become a major problem unless you know how to let them go.

One of the main benefits of using this approach is to get your thoughts and feelings flowing again. It also provides you with the tools to deal with the physical, mental and spiritual pain brought about by troublesome feelings, attitudes, thoughts and emotions. Regular practice will empower you and transform your life in a very short time. This means that troublesome thoughts and feelings will no longer be a source of chronic physical, mental and spiritual pain and discomfort for you.

***

Destroy the Inventory

When you have completed this emotional stocktaking exercise, do not leave your inventory lying around. Once you have read through it and shared what you need to share, then it needs to be destroyed. This is a major therapeutic element of the letting go process. One way to do this is to burn your inventory and watch it go up in smoke if you can. As it burns, say and repeat the following affirmation:

I now let go of all my troublesome thoughts and feelings.

Burning your inventory is a very powerful and symbolic way of letting go of old thoughts and feelings. You must now replace the old with the new to finish the job. This is simply done through the use of affirmations.

Replacing Emotional Liabilities with Assets

Use the following affirmations to replace the emotional assets and liabilities from your inventory:

I am clearheaded
I am loving
I am forgiving
I am patient
I am compassionate

Use these affirmations to practise step three and replace everything in your inventory.

You can also use each of these, or any other affirmation, as an independent exercise at any time. To do this say each affirmation a few times, pausing for about three seconds between each repetition. Say and repeat these affirmations often throughout the day.

Why Emotional Stocktaking?

The main purpose of doing an inventory of emotions and feelings is so that you know and deal with what goes on in your mind. This exercise will also help you identify your thoughts and feelings specifically, which is crucial to letting them go. They can then be replaced immediately through the use of affirmations.

Some troublesome thoughts and feelings can disguise themselves as a kind of normal presence in your life for many years. In some case they will stay around your whole life unless you take action to remove them. If they are not identified and removed, they can place serious limitations on your well-being and can even cause major mental, physical and spiritual problems.

The good news is that all these associated problems can be prevented. Prevention is the best cure for any ailment! So, even if you think you have no troublesome thoughts and feelings, do an emotional inventory and you will be amazed at what you discover about yourself and you will benefit from it.

The more you practise this exercise, the more it will reveal to you. Not only does it reveal your traits in the form of your emotional liabilities but it will also highlight your qualities in the form of emotional assets. It will allow you to have a more in-depth sharing experience and facilitate the replacement of old feelings, attitudes, thoughts, emotions and other old ideas that may be lurking about in your mind.

CHAPTER SEVEN

Helpful Ideas and Tips

As you continue on your journey towards happiness and peace of mind, you will grow in confidence as you begin to experience your own progress. You will also become more aware of the need to keep practising the core steps and the other exercises as they are introduced.

In this chapter, you will be introduced to other helpful ideas and tips to add to your overall personal development and well-being tool kit. These ideas and tips, like most of the other suggestions and exercises take only minutes to learn and seconds to apply, with a few exceptions. For instance, the emotional stocktaking exercise may take a few minutes longer to apply the first time you do it.

Also, some of the meditations introduced later in Chapter 14 will take more than a few minutes to practise in their entirety. Nevertheless, you can make them as long or as short as you want. If practised over a few months these meditations and the other exercises will start to become a spontaneous response to the stresses and strains of life. You will find them a safe place to go when you need a bit of quiet time or to recharge your batteries.

Set Your Mind to Zero

This idea was mentioned briefly in the previous chapter it will now be explained in a little more detail. To set your mind to zero, you will need to be able to turn off your feelings, attitudes, thoughts and emotions completely. This means being able to turn your mind off and turn it back on again. It is a bit like stopping and restarting your computer or mobile phone when it gets clogged up. Switching your computer or phone off for a few seconds then back on again has the effect of deleting some temporary files and freeing up your device when it is rebooted. Likewise, when you set your mind to zero, you will also be switching it off then back on again. This will clear unwanted feelings, attitudes, thoughts and emotions when you restart again. This will give a few valuable seconds to regain your composure.

How to Set Your Mind to Zero

The question is how? How do you set your mind to zero? The quickest and best way to do this is to do a Time Out. This is a very simple exercise and you can learn how to do this in Chapter 14. One other way to do this is to do an emotional inventory, make a list of your thoughts and feelings then apply the three steps.

You could also just use an affirmation. To do this close your eyes and listen for the silence then, after a few seconds, say:

I am aware of the silence I now set my mind at zero.

Spend no more than a few seconds doing this exercise. Each time you practise it will become easier and more effective.

After doing it for a number of months you will begin to see and experience silence and zero as being the same thing. A word of caution, if you have to stand when doing this exercise for example at work. or waiting for a bus hold on to something for support and keep your eyes open.

You can use this affirmation at any time at home or at work. Morning and night are always good times to use this or any affirmations. Keep in mind although affirmations will work on their own, they will always work best with the three steps. This exercise is like a stopwatch that allows you to set everything in your mind at zero and restart your life.

One Word

When you become fluent in the language of positive affirmations and healthy self-talk, you will actually arrive at a stage in your development where one word will suffice to bring about the desired change. For example, zero, silence, peace, happiness, joy, calm, stop and the like. The use of these and other words in your vocabulary is powerful. They become even more powerful when used with intent. Changing the kind of language used towards yourself and others is a very powerful and healthy practice to get into.

Using Affirmations

You can use affirmations at any time, during the day or night, at work or at play. Say and repeat them often as a set of affirmations or choose one and work with it on its own for a while. Affirmations can be used for virtually anything you are trying to achieve.

When practising affirmations, say them often, every hour of every day if you have to until they are part of your being. The idea is to get used to using powerful positive language. Eventually, you will be able to set everything in your life to zero by simply saying to yourself, "I now set everything in my life at zero."

Before you can do this, you will need to get used to using affirmative healthy language to yourself. A good way to do this is to memorise some of the affirmations in these pages and say them often. It is also good practice to create your own and use them as need them.

Tried and Tested

As you continue to move along on your journey and become more familiar with how this approach works, you will become more aware of what you need to do, to stay on course. The ideas expressed in this book are suggested as a guide to assist you on your way. They have been tried and tested ever since human beings began to think, feel and talk. They are the products of the wisdom of the past and are shared here to give you the confidence and help you need to continue on your way.

Knowledge is Power but…

Acquiring knowledge, as with all the other changes that you make in your life, will, at first, feel awkward and unfamiliar. The good news for you now is that the more you learn and discover, the less challenging it all becomes. The more knowledge you have, the more equipped you will be to deal with life's unknown unknowns. However, knowledge has its limitations: for example, knowledge is power only if it is applied. Otherwise, it is just useless information.

Avoiding Change

Some people will do anything to avoid change but the reality is, it cannot be avoided. Change does not require or ask for your consent. For example, as you grow, your physical body changes. As you continue to grow and get older, your body changes even more. Change cannot be stopped. You might be able to slow it down but it will continue to happen.

Many people try to resist change in whatever form it comes. These people belong to a group who would like to stay the way they are and try to get everyone else to change. Yet, change is the only thing that will always be there with you in your life. Therefore, although you cannot stop change, you do have a choice in how you respond to it.

Do you want misery in your life or do you want peace and happiness? If you want peace and happiness, you've got to accept change and go with it. This will bring contentment and inner peace into your life like you have never known before. Use the following affirmation if you feel you need to be more accepting of change in your life. You can also use it with the three core steps.

Say, *I accept change in my life right now.*

Repeat often!

When Change Starts to Happen

When you participate in any kind of activity, some part of you is going to change. Moreover, any action or activity you participate in is at some level, part of your personal development. You may not look at it like this but, that is what happens. Whether you are having a shower, going for a walk, going to school or college, or having a meal. This is all part of your ongoing personal development, your evolution as a human being and the change taking place in you and in your life. Before, during and after any activity, you are going to be different. Sometimes you may not be aware that you have changed because change can be very subtle.

Sometimes Obvious and Strange

Along with being subtle change will sometimes be obvious and strange. When you practise this approach to managing thoughts and feelings, correctly you will feel some changes. If you do not feel like you are changing after practising the steps for a reasonable period of time, you will need to go back to the quick guide and make sure you are practising correctly.

Remember, the first thing you need to do in this approach is the core three steps, exactly as they are written to get the desired results. As you practise with greater sincerity and willingness, you will begin to feel, appreciate, and eventually love the changes you are experiencing. Keep practising correctly and you will be well rewarded.

Some people accept and go through change as if it were something with which they were completely familiar. Others fight change as if it were the enemy. Use the following affirmation to help remove resistance to change.

Say, *The war is over for me. I accept change.*

Repeat often!

Is Change just for Everyone Else?

"Change is something you want everyone else to do."
– Louise L. Hay

There may be times in your life when you feel that the world would be a wonderful place if everyone else would change and do it your way. That may or may not be true. Either way, if you are putting your happiness and well-being on hold until everyone else falls into line with your thinking, you may be in for a long wait.

Your happiness and well-being are much too important to place in the hands of other people and their willingness to change. The key to happiness and peace of mind is to accept the change taking place in you and get on with living. Practise the following affirmation.

Say, *I accept change. I am now living my own life.*

Repeat often!

Change: The Only Constant

Change is a constant presence in life. Change is actually the only known constant in life you can rely on. It should not be feared or shunned. Even the laws of physics are not as constant, as was once thought. However, change is still a rock-solid constant and therefore needs to be acknowledged and accepted. So, no matter what is happening in your life right now, it will change. It may feel like it is never ending but it will change and pass.

The good news is that you will remain and possess the emotional and spiritual assets and qualities you cultivate throughout your life. Your peace of mind, happiness and overall well-being are dependent on how quickly you can adapt to change.

Why Me?

Why me? Why am I like this? Why can't I be happy? Why?

When dealing with feelings, attitudes, thoughts and emotions, these questions are actually not very helpful when it comes to providing a solution. The answers may provide interesting reading and more information for academics and researchers but will offer little in the form of a remedy for the person who needs relief.

If your boat is sinking and you are on board, it won't matter why it's sinking or who is to blame. What will matter is that you get to safety. Spending your precious time trying to find out why and who is to blame is not going to help save you.

Why or Who?

In reality, it does not really matter why or who. If you feel like you are in a sea of emotional turmoil and in danger of sinking, you need a lifeboat. One lifeboat available to you right now is this approach to well-being. With the three core steps at the helm, it will take you to the dry land of happiness and peace of mind if you use it.

Get into this lifeboat! You may not like having to use it but it is better than drowning in a sea of loneliness, fear and misery. If you find out why your boat sank after you are safe, great! For now, use your lifeboat until you are feeling safe and secure again.

By the way, this lifeboat will take you much farther than you expect. In fact, if you persevere, you will arrive on the shores of a land far beyond what you could ever have dreamed of when you started out on this journey.

Blaming the Past or Others

When life is going wrong, it is not unusual to start looking for something or someone to blame. However, blaming the past or others for the way you feel about your life right now will be of no benefit to you.

The reality is that there can be any number of reasons why you feel the way you do. Terrible things may have happened to you. They may still be happening but, if you want to have peace and happiness in your life, you will have to let go of blame and the continuous search for reasons "why" you feel so badly.

You do not need to know "why" bad things happen to you before you can find peace. Start practising the three core steps now and say goodbye to those bad feelings, attitudes, thoughts and emotions that keep you in a state of fear and unhappiness. Stick with the core steps and as many of the other practices in this approach and you will discover so much more as you continue your journey towards peace and happiness.

Absurd and a Waste of Time?

Naming troublesome thoughts and feelings will be absolutely no problem to some people. Some will instinctively know how to do it and know why they need to do it. To others, the whole idea of naming a thought or feeling will seem absurd and a waste of time.

There are also those who are so badly beaten by life that they will be willing to do whatever it takes, to find relief and comfort right from the start. If you are one of the 'badly beaten' you will start to experience the benefits of practising this approach immediately. This is simply because you are ready do whatever it takes to get on the road to peace of mind and happiness.

Do You Want to be Happy or Right?

Why should I acknowledge that anything is wrong? It's all those other people. If they would just leave me alone. Just stay out of my way and do it my way. I could get on with my life. You may be right!

It may be the rest of the human race that's out of step. Either way, you will still have to adapt to the situations that life presents to you. Otherwise, you will continue to be a very unhappy, miserable person while you wait for the world to change. The thing is, you may be right but if being right makes you unhappy, maybe you ought to consider another option.

The question you need to ask and answer is, do you want to be happy or right? If you want to be right at the expense of your happiness, that's your choice. On the other hand, if you want to be happy, give up the resistance, stop fighting life and get on the road to happiness and greater well-being. Don't forget, you can practise all your affirmations as part of the three steps.

Say, *I surrender. The war is over for Me. I now let go of all resistance.*

Repeat often!

Beating Resistance

The power and the tendency to challenge the conditions imposed on you by nature is part of what makes you a human being. Resistance is an essential requirement for the survival of humanity but has to be used wisely to be of benefit. For example fighting and resisting the changes you experience as you grow older is not wise because it will lead to a very sad old age. On the other hand acceptance of this kind of change will lead to your happiness and enjoyment of all your life including your old age. The best and simplest way to beat resistance is to stop fighting with it.

Say, *I surrender and accept change.*

Repeat often!

What is Well-Being?

What is well-being about? One way of understanding well-being is to see it as being all about your physical, mental and spiritual health. These three levels of your being are supported by faculties and powers that also need to be taken on board when considering well-being. These three levels of being are all central to your lasting well-being. For now though just consider well-being as having a knowing that all is well in your world at this moment in time.

Body, Mind, Spirit

No doubt you have seen the terms mind, body, spirit, written somewhere or heard somebody mention them in conversation. So, they may have a familiar ring to them. However, they are more than just trendy statements to toss around in conversation. They are the essential constituents that make human beings human beings. It is the interaction between these constituents that keep people alive and behaving like human beings. Nevertheless, as wonderful as they are, they are still only parts of what you are.

Body and Mind

The human body and mind do not have the ability to stay alive and work on their own, or even together. The body and mind are both dependent faculties. Simply put, your mind depends on a body with a brain which in turn depends on a planet called Earth. This planet depends on the sun, which depends on something else and so on. Therefore, there is a need for other faculties which allow you to tap into some kind of power or energy that keeps all the faculties working together. If you follow this logic, it is clear that there is more to you than meets the eye.

Energy, Power and Spirit

When you look at yourself in this light, you can see that you are much more than a body with a mind or, a combination of both. Your body and your mind are only parts of what you are. This is because they are both dependent on something else and each other.

As mentioned earlier, your body and mind need some other form of energy to keep them working together. For the purpose of this discussion, this power or energy will be called "the human spirit" and acts like a kind of "spiritual brain" in that it carries information to the mind to be acted on.

The human spirit does not depend on the body, the brain or the mind it simply connects you to another source of information, energy and power. It is the flow of this energy that keeps your body alive, your mind thinking and your heart beating and feeling.

Without the human spirit the energy that sustains you would not be able to flow into your life. If you are serious about your happiness and peace of mind explore these concepts further at every opportunity.

I Think Therefore I am Human

The three core steps are designed to help you manage and let go of troublesome thoughts and feelings. They are not designed to stop you from thinking. Having thoughts and feelings, troublesome or otherwise, is part of what makes you a human being.

It was basically this kind of thinking which led the French philosopher, René Descartes to say, "I think therefore I am." He could just as easily have said, "I think therefore I am a human being."

The point is that it is okay to think your thoughts. The capacity to think, comprehend and act on your thoughts are among the distinguishing characteristics that make human beings what they are.

This capacity also brings with it the responsibility to act in accordance with human values; otherwise, it will bring misery into your life. This is the main reason why you need to be able to manage your thinking, along with your feelings, attitudes and emotions.

Practise Gratitude

The practice of gratitude is also something that you should develop. This is so simple to do that you can do it right now. For example, let's say you want to practise gratitude for having peace of mind:

Say, *I am grateful for my peace of mind right now*.

Repeat often and don't forget to pause for a few seconds between repetitions! You can also try to create your own gratitude affirmations starting with the words:

I am grateful for _____

Following on from this you can also write a gratitude list. This is very simple and effective. To make a gratitude list, you will need a pen and paper. Next write a simple list of what you are grateful for as follows:

I am grateful for my life
I am grateful for my food I am grateful for...

The practice of making a gratitude list can be done at any time: for example, when it is difficult to see any good in the world. It is also especially beneficial to do a gratitude list when you are at peace with yourself.

Fault Finding

Fault finding is a very unhelpful practice and needs to be avoided. It is sinister in that it can occur consciously and unconsciously. If it is allowed to continue in your life, it will condemn you to a life of sadness and unhappiness. Fault finding is the practice of looking at what is wrong with others and in the world around you. Yes, there are things happening in the world that are not perfect.

Some of these you can change and some of them, you have no control over. All the complaining, blaming and crying will not change them. If you are really serious about changing and transforming your life for good, you have got to let the practice of fault finding go. If you catch yourself making a negative statement about anything or anyone, immediately say to yourself, STOP!

STOP!

STOP is a powerful word and a great tool to have when you need a quick remedy. Along with using it to eliminate fault finding, you can also use it to help prevent other unwanted thoughts and feelings from taking control of you. You can use it in times of panic for example, if you begin to feel afraid and overwhelmed command the fear to stop. To do this, in your mind you must forcibly tell the fear to STOP. If you are alone for example at home you can say this out loud. If you are in a crowd you will have to do this silently in your mind. You may have to do this a number of times but persevere and you will get relief. The word STOP and the other suggestions work best along with the core steps not instead of them.

Friends

In these days of the COVID-19 lockdown, most of your contact with friends will be through the use of technology. However, as soon as the lockdown finishes and the world resumes its natural activities, it will be time to reconnect physically. The lockdowns have shown that it is vitally important to have social contacts and people in your life you can meet and talk with

Friends come in many shapes and forms. Sometimes you will have friends through circumstances for example, people you went to school or college with, work colleagues and other acquaintances. Most of these friendships will come to an end when you finish school, college or when the job ends. There will also be friendships that withstand the test of time and other issues. Among your friends you may even find someone to share with and be able to develop a deeper bond of fellowship.

Developing Friendships

When you are developing these kinds of friendships, you will obviously need to meet like-minded people. The best way to do this is become the kind of person you would like to be with.

Ask yourself, do you have a good relationship with yourself? Do you like spending time with yourself? If the answer is no, then you need to change this, you will need to build a relationship with yourself. When you have a relationship with yourself and you like spending time with yourself, then others will want to spend time with you. The first step in relationship building is to build a relationship with yourself first.

To start building a relationship with yourself first make a list of the qualities you would like to see in a person you would like as a friend or companion. Your qualities list may include kindness, compassion, empathy and patience. Next, start cultivating and developing these qualities in yourself. Then you will start to attract that kind of person into your life.

Letting Go of Traits

When you are building relationships with yourself and others using this method, the likelihood is that you will also need to let go of unpleasant human traits. These are characteristics that you do not want to see in the people whom you want to have a relationship with. These traits may include selfishness, coldness, self-centredness and intolerance.

Use the three core steps to let go of any unwanted traits you have identified in yourself. If you haven't done this kind of work on yourself before, it will feel a bit strange. However, you will quickly come to enjoy spending time with yourself. Then, others will actually seek out your company.

Self-Love

If you are completely new to the idea of loving yourself, the chances are you will have to make some changes to the way you have treated yourself up to this time in your life. For example, you may have difficulty saying something like, "I love myself". You may not even be able to say you like yourself.

The trouble with this attitude is that if you don't begin to like and love yourself, you will not be able to like and love anyone else. Real friendship and fellowship require unconditional love first, for "yourself" then, for others and beyond that the world around you.

Remember, when you begin to take care of yourself in this way you will begin to attract people into your life who are capable of loving you and you will also be capable of loving them.

More to You

There is much 'more to you' than your physical existence: you also have feelings, attitudes, thoughts and emotions to deal with. Along with these you also have the ability to understand, make decisions, use your imagination, store and recall information to mention but a few. These are the facilities that make you human and therefore special in the world of being. These physical and mental capabilities are part of the material side of your being. This brings with it something that can cause great difficulty for some human beings that is, the freedom of choice.

Because you are a human being, at a certain time in your life you acquire the capacity to make choices. The choices and especially the moral choices you make affect your feelings, attitude, thoughts and emotions. They have a direct impact on your happiness, peace of mind and overall well-being. These choices will also have an enormous effect on your physical well-being.

The great news for you now is that, if you have been practising the three steps and at least some of the other suggestions, by now you will have more control over the choices you make. This means you are taking responsibility for your own well-being and happiness. This is a sign of great progress.

Values and Choices

Keep in mind that your well-being and happiness are directly connected to the moral choices you make in relation to how you respond to the everyday events in your life. The reason for this is that you have a set of values or morals that you live by. Everyone has! If you act outside your values or moral choices it will greatly reduce your peace of mind and overall well-being.

The choice and responsibility of living within these standards is yours. These values and morals are partly inherited from the society or culture you are born into. Whether you like it or not you are expected to abide by them for the greater good. If you choose not to abide by the values of your society, you may have to bear the pain of personal shame and guilt. In some societies, a breach of the standard morals and values may even cost you your life. You can see how this might not be good for your overall happiness and well-being.

Deeper Values

There are deeper values, however, that have a more profound effect on your well-being and happiness than the standards of any society. These are your own personal values and morals. For example, if you break the law of the society that you live in, you may find yourself in trouble with the authorities. However, if you act outside the standards you have set for yourself, the penalties are not so obvious but can be even more detrimental to your well-being.

In the case of societal standards, you have no choice but to obey them but when it comes to your own standards and values, you have the choice. The upshot of this is that you can choose to be happy or miserable. If you choose to live your life within the standards and values set by you and the society in which you live you will have peace of mind. Choosing to act outside these value systems will leave you feeling miserable and this will not be good for your overall happiness and well-being.

To avoid unhappiness and misery try to act and behave at least within your own personal values. This is one of the keys to happiness and peace of mind. Having said that remember, no one is perfect everyone slips and falls. What's important is that when you fall you get up and continue your journey.

A Matter of Choice

It really is a matter of choice and this is a choice only you can make. You have the power to control your feelings, attitudes, thoughts and emotions but if you let them, they will control you.

It has been mentioned, several times, that this is a simple approach to managing thoughts and feelings. You may not agree with this right now but the more you practise the suggestions, the more you will come to realise that this is true. It may take a bit of time to get the exercises under your belt but remember, you do not have to learn or practise them all together. The best way to advance on any journey is to take it step by step.

Once you have taken the three core steps and memorised them, you will be able to apply them as needed. You can then work your way through the rest of the approach gradually. Although it takes only minutes to memorise each of the individual exercises and seconds to apply them, it may take a bit of time to become familiar with all of them. The point to remember here is that managing your thoughts and feelings is simple once you know how. If you are willing to change and make a sincere effort to apply the suggestions, you are already halfway there.

These practices will help you to become more knowledgeable about yourself and open a door into the wonderful world of wisdom and understanding. This door will open suddenly for many!

CHAPTER EIGHT

Step One – a bit deeper

Name It

Over the next three chapters, the three core steps are explored and discussed on a deeper level. You will gain a greater knowledge of what is actually taking place when you practise the steps and take on board the other suggestions. As you move through the different stages of your personal development, this knowledge and understanding will ensure you stay on the right path.

These deepening discussions are to help advance your understanding of the three steps which are like a door into another world. When you apply and begin to experience the steps on a deeper level, you will become more aware of your own well-being improving and you will be cultivating and guaranteeing your continued peace of mind and happiness into the future.

Admitting, Acknowledging, Identifying

As with anything you do, when you first do it there are certain things you will not know or need to know. For example, when you first drive a car, you don't need to know how to change a wheel, put water in the windscreen washer or fuel in the tank. However, you quickly realise that if you don't learn how to do these things you won't get very far. It is exactly the same when it comes to the steps the more you know about them the more you will benefit from using them.

When you begin to practise the three steps for the first time you will not be aware of what is actually happening. For example, when you are naming a troublesome feeling, attitude, thought or emotion, there are a number of very important underlying things happening:

Admitting
Acknowledging
Identifying

This is just three of the things that occur when you are doing step one. More than likely you will not have been aware of any of these when you started out, either way, it's now time for a deeper exploration of the steps. They may or may not happen in the order they are listed here but they are happening. For example, you may identify a troublesome thought or feeling before you admit or acknowledge it as yours. Likewise you may admit or acknowledge a feeling before you can identify it specifically. However, they will be discussed as they are listed.

Admitting

The first underlying thing to be discussed when naming troublesome thoughts or feelings is that you are admitting to yourself that you are having them. There is nothing negative or wrong about having any kind of thoughts and feelings, regardless of what they are, so long as you know how to manage them. Yet it can be very difficult to do especially if you have to admit it to someone else. In the context of the first step admitting is very much a private matter. This means that you are only admitting to yourself privately.

At this stage, you know something is wrong but you may not know exactly what it is. For example, you may not yet know that you are stressed, anxious or lonely. All you know is something does not feel right. To admit, at this stage, might be something like saying to yourself, "I don't feel right. Something is wrong." Remember this is not naming the thought or feeling yet it is just admitting something is wrong.

Easy for Some

For some people admitting to yourself that you are having a troublesome thought or feeling will be very easy to do, for others, it will be more of a challenge. One reason for this is that some people (dare I say, in particular, men) tend to see an admission of any kind as a form of weakness. Thankfully, this is changing as both women and men are becoming more willing to talk about their thoughts and feelings.

Cautious Move

When you are learning how to manage your thoughts and feelings, it is important to be aware that you will, more often than not, be doing the opposite to what you normally do in your day-to-day life. For example, in the normal course of events in your life you probably wouldn't admit to yourself let alone anyone else that you are anxious or afraid.

Admitting something even to yourself can be a challenge. It may be because it is your first time dealing with issues relating to your thoughts and feelings. Be patient with yourself! Some of these thoughts and feelings will have a greater hold on your life than you may have realised. As you become more familiar with this approach to wellbeing, the practice of naming, sharing and replacing those sticky thoughts and feelings will get much easier even enjoyable.

Acknowledging

Another underlying thing that happens when naming a thought or feeling is that you are acknowledging something needs to be addressed. In reality this is simply an acknowledgement that something in particular is wrong. It is more of a face-to-face encounter with a particular issue. You know it's there; you will not have specifically identified it yet but you can feel it or you are thinking it. There may even be a sense of relief at this point because you are no longer avoiding the issue.

During the practice of step one, when you admit something is wrong, you will be partly acknowledging it. Likewise, when acknowledging something has to change, there will be an element of admitting taking place.

First Contact

Just like admitting, acknowledging may be your first real and conscious contact with fear, anxiety, stress or other troublesome thoughts and feelings therefore, it will feel uncomfortable. You may, in fact, not want to have any contact with them at all. This is a perfectly natural reaction and to be expected. Unfortunately, it leads many people to ignore their feelings, attitude, thoughts and emotions completely and as a result, they are unable to deal with them at all. Therefore, any kind of an acknowledgement of a feeling is a good start but, it will need to be a bit more specific to be of real benefit.

Sign of Well-Being

It is very important that you are also aware that acknowledging a troublesome thought or feeling is a sign of well-being. For example, if someone shares with you that they are feeling sad, unhappy, lonely and afraid remember, this is actually a sign of wellness. This kind of acknowledgement is a giant step in dealing with and letting go of troublesome feelings, attitudes, thoughts and emotions. If a person is willing and wants to let go of those feelings altogether, they simply need to be as specific as possible and continue with the other two steps.

Acknowledgement and Denial

Unfortunately when faced with troublesome thoughts and feelings, the last thing that most people want to do is acknowledge them. Denial offers no protection against the onslaught of a troubled mind yet this is the first line of defence used by many. They hope that in some way by ignoring the issue it will somehow disappear and go away.

Sadly, all that happens is that troublesome thoughts and feelings multiply and quickly become unmanageable. Acknowledging and admitting relieves much of the emotional pain and mental anguish associated with denial. During the process of naming, acknowledging and admitting allow troublesome thoughts and feelings to be captured and later let go during the practice of step two.

Acknowledgement and Isolation

Acknowledgement is not something to be conducted in isolation. This means that acknowledgement is part of a bigger picture. For example, there is no point in acknowledging a troublesome thought or feeling and doing nothing about it. Acknowledgement must be followed by the action of the rest of the process, otherwise you will have acknowledged what's wrong but nothing will change. If you half do it, the only thing that will happen is that you will feel bad and you'll know why. As you can see that will be of little comfort and changes nothing.

Acknowledging the Correct Feeling

Another point of huge importance in relation to naming a fear is that you must acknowledge the correct feeling. For example, the fear of flying is a fairly common topic of conversation. This feeling makes life very difficult for some people. The way to manage it is to name it, share it and replace it. However, the steps will only work if you have acknowledged and named the correct feeling.

Is it flying that you are afraid of? Is this a true statement? In many cases, when the "I'm afraid of flying" statement is examined, it is often found to be incorrect. Many people mix up a fear of flying with a fear of dying. The main reason this fear is so difficult to deal with is that the wrong feeling is being acknowledged. On closer examination it is often found that the real fear is, dying in a plane crash.

To deal with any kind of feeling, it is absolutely essential to acknowledge the correct feeling.

Flying or Dying?

If someone is trying to deal with the fear of flying the question should be asked; is it the fear of flying or is it the fear of dying in a plane crash? This question must be answered correctly otherwise, the actual fear cannot be dealt with. If, as in this scenario, the fear is dying in a plane crash and the person refuses to accept this, then the fear cannot be dealt with. This is simply because the real fear is not being acknowledged and therefore cannot be named, shared and replaced.

When you are dealing with any feeling, attitude, thought or emotion you must name it specifically. Remember you are dealing with something intangible this means, you will not be able to see it or touch it in the physical sense. The only real way to manage intangibles such as feelings, attitudes, thoughts and emotions is to take hold of them figuratively speaking, then, let them go. This action takes place in your mind where these decisions are made.

Subtle Self-Deception

It is absolutely essential, when dealing with feelings, attitude thoughts and emotions that you are as specific and as accurate as possible. This will strengthen the functionality of the steps and make them more effective.

Obviously as in the "I am afraid of flying" statement in the previous example, there is no intention to mislead. Nevertheless, this statement is very misleading, it is a very subtle case of self-deception and denial but it is not unusual. It will happen at some stage in life to most people. It is a tactic of the human mind used to avoid dealing with situations that are too unpleasant to face head on.

Substituting one fear for another is a common enough practice. The problem is if you allow self-deception to go on, it will make it very difficult or even impossible to deal with the actual fear effectively. The next underlying feature of step one is the idea of identifying specifically what the troublesome thought or feeling is.

Identifying

In this chapter the discussion is exploring in depth what happens when you are naming troublesome thoughts or feelings in the context of the three steps. Three underlying features of the first step are being discussed. Up to now admitting and acknowledging thoughts and feelings have been discussed. You can now explore the idea of identifying a thought or feeling specifically.

As with the other parts of the first step specifically identifying thoughts and feelings is essential before you can let them go. Also you need to know exactly what you are actually doing when you are practising the steps otherwise you will not get the benefit of your efforts.

Identifying a feeling, attitude, thought or emotion for the purpose of letting it go requires you to be as specific as possible. You will notice that the word specific keeps cropping up in this discussion. This is because it is absolutely crucial. The more specific you are, the more successful you will be.

To be specific also means that you will have to be completely honest with yourself because if you try to fool yourself, there is no hope of dealing with troublesome thoughts and feelings. You are the only person who will actually know how self-honest you are and you will be reminded of this in the way you feel as time goes by.

True to Yourself
You've got to be true to yourself or at least willing to be. The measure of how true to yourself, you have been, will be seen in the results. In other words, your overall wellbeing will largely depend on how truthful and honest you are with yourself.

Self-honesty is one of the essentials of this approach. Without this ingredient, it will not work. Self-honesty when dealing with troublesome thoughts and feelings means you are accountable only to yourself.

This will allow you to be as specific as possible when identifying exactly what it is that's causing the problem. The more specific you are, the more successful you will be. When you are true to yourself the more happiness and well-being will come into your life.

Being honest and true to yourself will have the effect of opening a channel through which flows the happiness and contentment you desire.

What Do You Mean?

So, the question arises; what do you mean? If, for example, you identify feelings and thoughts as follows; "I feel stressed" or "I feel lonely" or "I am thinking about dying" this is a good place to start but you will need to do a bit more exploring to find out exactly what it is you mean.

What does 'stressed' mean? Is it just anxiety that you are feeling? Does it mean fear? Are you afraid?

Likewise what do you mean by lonely? Does it mean you are on your own? Do you feel lonely in a crowd?

Again, what do you mean by dying? Is it the process of dying that you are thinking about? Maybe it is death itself that you are thinking about?

These questions need to be answered honestly so that when you practise step two you will be able to let go completely of whatever it is that bothers you. It is important too that you realise that the actual letting go begins the minute you start to practise step one. The more specific you are when identifying what's wrong the quicker you will be able to "name it" and let it go.

More Specific

Say, for example, you are afraid of dogs. At first, you might say, "I am afraid of dogs."

How can you be more specific? You may be afraid of specific types of dogs, in which case, you could say for example, "I am afraid of pit bull terriers." Now you are getting more specific!

Again remember the more specific you are, the greater the benefit will be to you. This applies when dealing with all feelings, attitudes, thoughts and emotions.

Scary

Sometimes the thought or feeling that you are dealing with is so scary, you will not even want to mention its name. In other words, you will not want to admit it or acknowledge it, let alone identify it specifically.

At first, you can identify the feeling or thought generally then, as you move towards the feeling, you will be able to acknowledge and identify it more specifically. In this way, you will be able to gradually approach the fear and name it specifically.

Once you get to the point where you can say to yourself, "I am afraid of…" followed by, "I am now letting go of…" then you are ready to share and let go.

Language

Before going on, there are a few more essentials you should not lose sight of in relation to, not just the first step but all three. First the language you use to yourself has an enormous effect on every part of your life. The words you use in your daily interactions with yourself and others have an enormous effect on how you think and feel. The first conscious response to troublesome feelings, attitudes, thoughts and emotions is usually with words. For example you might say something to yourself like, "No, not this again" or, "I hate this feeling". As you read on, you will see that this kind of self-talk is very unhelpful.

Keep in mind that your words are powerful tools when it comes to managing thoughts and feelings. For example, in the previous chapter, the word STOP was mentioned in relation to dealing with panic and emotional outbursts. When practising the steps, words will be on the front line of contact with your feelings and emotions therefore, you will need to become more mindful of the language and words you use.

Unhelpful Sayings

Now that you know the language you use is very powerful, using unhelpful words and phrases to yourself should be avoided. These include: "I can't do it", "yah but", "I'm not able", "It's too difficult for me", "I don't believe it", among others. Unfortunately, these have become all too common and they need to be removed from your vocabulary.

They offer no help at all to your progress and will hold you back in all areas of your life if you don't stop using them. These sayings and unhelpful language will be very detrimental to your well-being and may even stop your progress altogether. Continued use of this kind of language will ensure that you will never achieve your goals, destroy your self-esteem and remove any semblance of happiness you may have.

What to Use Instead

The situations you face in life will always involve feelings, attitudes, thoughts and emotions. In managing these situations, the importance of the language you use and your internal self-talk cannot be overstated. If you use unhelpful language like that mentioned above you will have to change this practice.

Instead of *I can't* say, *I can*. Instead of *yah but* say, *yah, (no buts)*. Instead of *I'm not able* say, *I am able*.

This is a very simple solution but it really works. From now on remember the words and language you use to yourself and everyone else have a major impact on how successful you will be in achieving your goals.

***

Wisdom of the Past

Everything in this book is really just the wisdom of the past presented with the benefit of hindsight. This hindsight spans thousands of years, during which time, mankind has been continually advancing towards an ever-evolving maturation. So, in one sense there is nothing original here yet in another, everything is new and fresh. This is because change is unceasing and with each passing moment everything in existence is being transformed and renewed.

A Progression

The three steps are presented as a progression. They follow a pattern and need to be practised in this order to get the result you want. In other words they need to be practised as they are set out, otherwise little or no progress will be made.

Material Level

The three steps will work only on the material level of your being. This is simply because that is what they are designed for. The material level of being, in this discussion, is simply the physiological and the psychological level of your existence.

If you believe that your tangible material life is your only level of existence, then that is where you will benefit from the application of the steps. On the other hand if you believe that there is more to you than a body with a brain then for you the steps will be a path to the next level of your existence.

At some point in your journey, you will have to make a choice on whether you want to develop yourself as just a material being or as a spiritual being. What you decide will have an enormous effect on the level of contentment you enjoy in your life.

The Need for Understanding

When you are practising the steps, you will not be thinking of them as consisting of different parts. Each will simply be seen as just one step. However, as you continue to evolve and develop in your life, so too will your fundamental need to understand what you are doing and why you are doing it. This follows a basic pattern in human needs theory, which suggests that once one need is satisfied, human beings then move on to satisfy whatever their next need is.

Sooner or later, you will need to know how and why this approach works. This may be for your own personal reasons or, some other purpose. Satisfying the need for understanding or at least moving in the direction of satisfying this need brings about a since of achievement, fosters self-esteem and energises your overall personal development. This understanding has nothing to do with collecting information or academic qualifications – it is about acquiring wisdom.

Passing on Your Knowledge

As you continue to practise the steps your thinking will begin to expand beyond yourself and you will begin to see the wisdom in the sharing of your knowledge and your experiences. When you share your knowledge and life experience with other human beings your own transformation is greatly advanced and your sense of well-being is multiplied. To be able to help others, you must first be able to help yourself. This brings to mind a truism, "You cannot give what you haven't got."

If, for example, you want to pass on knowledge, then you must have knowledge to pass on. You will acquire information in this book but to turn this information into knowledge and wisdom you will need to practise the steps and the other suggestions in every area of your life.

As you make your way along the road to peace and happiness, exploring and practising as you go, you will find your knowledge and wisdom increasing. This will only happen when you are aware and know exactly what you are doing as you practise the steps. This is why these discussions are absolutely necessary.

Just a Reminder

You would be forgiven, as you continue this journey towards happiness and contentment for thinking that all this is very complicated but actually, it is not. The application of the three steps and all the other suggestions in this book, never changes and remains very simple to practise. If you stick with it, you will become more enlightened and your understanding of what's happening will change as the discussions and your practice continues.

As you are working your way through the broader reaches of this approach, you will start to experience a knowing. For some people, this experience will stay the first time it comes. For others, it will come and go for a period of time before it finally settles with you.

Understanding exactly what is happening when you are practising the three steps and indeed, the whole approach, can take a bit of getting used to. These discussions will help you see the bigger picture.

CHAPTER NINE

Step Two – a bit deeper

Share It

Step two is no different from the other two steps in that it is easy to learn and simple to apply. However, understanding how and why it works requires exploration and consideration. Therefore like anything else you are trying to master you will have to learn about it, memorise it and practise it until you can spontaneously apply it. In other words apply the four principles of mastery.

This deeper level of exploration will help you through those times when you might be tempted to stray off course and maybe go back to the old way of thinking. There may not be a precise answer to the 'how' and the 'why' questions but, by going into a deeper level of discussion, the insight you develop will enable you to walk the road of your life with more confidence. It will engrave upon your being the knowledge that you now have the tools to change your fate and make clear the way ahead.

To Recap!

The more you learn about and practise the steps correctly, the more you become aware of what you are actually doing. These discussions will help speed up the learning process. So far you have explored what happens when you practise the first step. That is, when you "name it", you are admitting, acknowledging and identifying your feelings, attitude, thoughts and emotions. Next the discussion will examine what happens when you begin to practise sharing in step two.

Magnetic Energy

When you start to practise sharing you will probably feel a little awkward and a bit unsure of yourself at first. You may even try to resist doing it altogether but this lack of familiarity will quickly pass if you stick with it. With a little practice, sharing will become as normal to you as breathing. This is because human beings are social beings and sharing is a very natural thing to do with each other.

In fact sharing is the foundation of fellowship and is the essential attracting influence of everything human. Furthermore, sharing between human beings is like a magnetic energy that keeps all human relationships together. This means that it is not just talking about a problem and it is definitely not talking about other people's problems. Step two is all about accepting your own thoughts and feelings and sharing exactly what they are with someone else for the purpose of letting them go.

Much More than Talking

The importance of sharing cannot be overstated! As was just mentioned, sharing is about much more than just talking about your thoughts and feelings. It is about handing it over to someone else, lightening the load, nullifying loneliness, isolation, fear and all kinds of emotional misery. It is about letting go. It is about freedom peace of mind, fellowship, love and so much more.

For you now, at this moment, it may be about reducing your level of anxiety, stress or suffering brought about by troublesome thoughts and feelings, with the ultimate goal of letting them go altogether.

Sharing can involve all sorts of communication such as body language, sign language, writing, texting, e-mail, written letters, listening, speaking, even silence. Sharing is actually one of the most amazing, underused personal development tools available to you.

A Problem Shared

Remember that old saying, "A problem shared is a problem halved"? Well, that is literally true, especially when it comes to thoughts and feelings. Furthermore when you share that same problem again, it is halved again.

As you continue to make sharing a regular part of your life, you will find that troublesome thoughts and feelings will lose their power over you. They will virtually evaporate.

As with step one, when you have been practising step two for a while, you will start to become aware of a number of underlying features. Three of these are now explored to help deepen your understanding of the step and how it works:

Accepting
Articulating
Letting go

Accepting

After practising the steps for a while you will begin to recognise and accept that all your thoughts and feelings are actually yours! They belong to you. At this moment, you may not want to accept this. Over time, you will realise the benefits of accepting your own thoughts and feelings and your own reality. As you practise the steps, your acceptance will gradually grow. So, although you may not be ready to accept all your thoughts and feelings just yet, you will at least have begun to. To help you on your way with acceptance say:

I accept all my thoughts and feelings now. Repeat often!

The Bridge of Acceptance

Acceptance is a higher level of awareness and allows you to break free from the chains of the blame game. It is like a bridge across a treacherous river. The idea of acceptance of your own thoughts and feelings is fundamental to letting them go and crossing that river.

Remember, you can't let go of something you do not have or you do not hold. This means that if you do not accept your own thoughts and feelings, you will not be able to let them go. So, saying and repeating, *I accept my thoughts and feelings*, is an essential element of letting them go.

As you become more comfortable saying this general affirmation, start becoming more specific. For example, if you are trying to accept a specific fear, like the fear of the dark:

Say, *I accept my fear of the dark. I am now letting this fear go.* Repeat often!

Practising Acceptance

Remember to practise acceptance say and repeat often, "I accept all my own thoughts and feelings". Then get specific. For example, when dealing with a specific feeling:

Say, *I accept my own fear of the dark.*

It is good practice to say something like "I am now letting go of these thoughts and feelings" after you practise acceptance.

If you are trying to accept a really difficult thought for example, around death:

Say, *I accept my thinking around death and I am now letting go of these thoughts.*

Acceptance will eventually play a major role in all of the steps and is paramount to letting go of all thoughts and feelings.

Taking Responsibility

Acceptance is akin to taking responsibility for your own fate. This does not mean that the painful situations in your life should be ignored, or that the people who did you wrong are not guilty of what they did. It means that you no longer allow these situations or people to have power over you.

By accepting your own thoughts and feelings around past events you prevent long gone experiences from continuing to hurt you. This will allow you to deal with them quickly. It will accelerate your progress towards greater well-being and peace of mind. It will help strengthen your mental health and put you in a better position to take any future actions you need to protect your peace of mind.

Before You Share

Remember to manage feelings, attitudes, thoughts and emotions they first have to be named. When you are naming them, you will also be admitting, acknowledging and identifying them as being yours. This is what you are actually doing when you are practising the first step. Once this step is done, you immediately move on to step two and are now holding the troublesome feeling, attitude, thought or emotion in your grasp. As you start to apply step two acceptance begins to kick in as you take ownership of your own thoughts and feelings.

The more acceptance you have before you share the easier it will be to be specific and clear about what you are sharing. It will also make it easier to articulate your thoughts and feelings during the practice of step two.

Articulating

Articulating is as simple as saying as specifically and clearly as possible, what it is that is troubling you. It involves breaking the silence and sharing what you are thinking and feeling with another person for the purpose of letting go completely. You have probably heard it said, 'silence is the silent killer'. Silence around certain kinds of thoughts and feelings will result in many people living and dying in misery. This need not happen.

This is why articulating and verbalising your troublesome thoughts and feelings as specifically as possible is so important, especially around the area of self-harm and suicide. This can be a very difficult issue to come to terms with but now you have the remedy. Sharing which involves the articulation of troublesome thoughts and feelings with the right kind of people is at the core of this remedy.

Expose the Silent Issues

Suicide is definitely one of the silent issues and needs to be exposed and shared. For some people, even to see the word suicide written down brings about fear, sadness and anxiety. You need not be afraid any longer because, to deal with any fears or anxiety around self-harm or suicide, all you need to do right now is name it, share it and replace it. If you can't find someone to share with, contact the helplines to share immediately. You do not need to let this bully have power over you any longer. You will find contact details for helplines in Chapter 2.

Someone to Share With

Finding someone to share your thoughts and feelings with is mentioned many times throughout this book because it is absolutely essential if you want to have peace of mind. If you decide not to share on the helplines make sure that whoever you share with is trustworthy and at least willing to learn about the steps so that they know what you are doing. The ideal situation is that the person you share with is also willing to practise the steps.

It is preferable that this person is not a member of your own family although, there are exceptions to this suggestion. The reason why it may not be advisable to share with family members is that they may be too close to you for the issues you want to share. Of course, you should share with your loved ones but, for very deep-rooted, sensitive issues, it is probably best to share with someone outside of your family who understands what you are trying to do.

So, Who Can You Share With?

Finding someone to share and articulate with can be a challenge and obviously, you need someone you can trust, so that you can complete the practice of step two. If you are in any doubt about someone, do not share with them. The good news is that you do not have to wait or put off the practice of step two while you are waiting to find a person to share with. Remember the free helplines are available anytime, day or night where you can share and remain completely anonymous. Therefore if you need someone to share with right now, please use them.

Many Helplines

Remember there are many helplines but contacting Samaritans is particularly beneficial if you are dealing with thoughts around self-harm and suicide but, you do not have to be suicidal to use this service. Any kind of troublesome thoughts or feelings can be shared on this helpline. Samaritans is not the only helpline available to you remember a comprehensive list of helplines is available at **www.suicidestop.com**

Information on other self-help groups can also be found in your local community. These groups can be very helpful and supportive until you find someone to share with on a one-to-one basis. In the meantime, do not hesitate to contact helplines most of them have text numbers along with e-mail addresses and can be contacted from anywhere around the world. They will be glad you contacted them. However, in the long run you will want to meet someone you can trust for the purpose of sharing and developing the bond of fellowship.

Therapists, Counsellors, Psychotherapists
Because of the intimate and confidential nature of sharing, you have to be sure that you are sharing with someone who is kind, compassionate and trustworthy. It is also absolutely essential that you know that the person you share with will keep your confidence. This is why a number of options are presented and made available to you.

Some of the other options available to you, involves using professionals such as therapists, counsellors or psychotherapists. There are also life coaches who may be willing to work with you on this.

Whoever you choose to work with, you will need to be able to tell them what it is you want to achieve. Remember too, if you choose to work with a professional, you are hiring them and there will be a cost involved.

How to Choose and Where to Find a Professional
A real professional will understand and know exactly what it is you are trying to achieve. If you are going for

an appointment, bring a copy of this book if you like and explain what it is you are doing. If you are talking with a real professional, they will understand what you are doing and will work with you. If he or she does not want to work with you on this basis, then that person is probably not a good fit for you. You may need to find someone else.

You can also check out professional help online. Most counsellors, psychologists, therapists and life coaches will have an online presence. This means that you can also have your sessions with your chosen professional online. In these days of COVID-19 that's as close as you are probably going to get to a face to face with a therapist until the pandemic ends.

The Right One for You

If you approach someone and they are not willing to listen to what you propose, then they will not be able to listen properly when you need to share. Sharing will ultimately be at the core of any remedy that works when dealing with thoughts and feelings.

Although, as professional practitioners in the field of emotional and general well-being they may have excellent qualifications, services or packages to offer remember, that is not what you are looking for right now. As you are now taking responsibility for your own wellbeing and as this undertaking will require at least one other person, you have to choose that person wisely.

Life coaching is an interesting one and may have what you might need but again, you must make sure, in so far as it is possible, to find the practitioner who is the right fit for you. Research it online and off and be patient. You may already know someone who fits the bill.

Letting Go

The final feature to be discussed about step two is "letting go". As you know, the second step is about sharing your troublesome feelings, attitudes, thoughts and emotions for the purpose of letting them go.

Strange as it may seem, some people get attracted to their troublesome thoughts and feelings. Some may even be fatally attracted to them and refuse to let them go. This is ultimately a matter of choice. Remember, it is your choice to let your troublesome thoughts and feelings go. Since you are still reading this, you have made the decision to let go or show someone else how to let go.

A Subject that Involves Everyone

How to manage your thoughts and feelings around the subject of suicide is addressed a number of times throughout this book for many reasons. The most important of these reasons is to "name it", "share it" and finally "replace it" because this is actually the solution!

The "naming" of self-harm and suicide will bring them out of the silence where they thrive. The "sharing" will release them and let them go. The "replacing" will replace them with peace of mind and contentment. The only other option is to ignore them in which case they will grow in the silence and continue to bring misery.

For those who are suicidal; those who think about suicide; those who may have a friend or relative who has taken their own life, knowing how to manage your thoughts and feelings around suicide is life transforming. Because these can be among the most troubling thoughts and feelings a human being has to deal with. The reality of this subject is that there are very few human beings on the planet who are not affected by it.

The good news is that you now have an answer. If you know of someone dealing with issues around self-harm show them how to use the three steps. Share this message of hope with them and others. Get the message out there so that people can find relief. Imagine what it must be like to be in their shoes.

If one life is saved or made a little less painful by your efforts it will be worth it. When you know how to deal with troublesome thoughts and feelings of any kind your life will change immeasurably. If you have been troubled by issues around self-harm, practise the three steps and you will know a freedom that you never thought possible.

Letting Go of a Suicidal Feeling

To let go of feelings around suicide you will need to name, share and replace them. This means you will have to be very specific about what you are feeling. This can be a difficult thing to do simply because firstly you will not want to name it, not to mention share it. However, once you do you will be free. The following exercise will help get you started. Let's say you are actually feeling suicidal. Say:

> **Name it**: *I am feeling suicidal. I am now letting go of this feeling.*
> **Share it**: *I am feeling suicidal. I am now letting go of this feeling.*
> **Replace it**: *I am safe and secure at all times. Repeat!*

When doing step two share exactly what's written. Practise the steps until the feeling subsides.

If you have someone to share with, that's great. If not, again it is strongly recommended that you ring or contact one of the helplines. This is mentioned very often throughout this book but it is because it is so important especially when dealing with thoughts and feelings around suicide.

Calling a Helpline

Some helplines, like Samaritans, were set up specially to allow people to share their thoughts and feelings around self-harm and suicide. To share, on the phone with a Samaritan volunteer first dial the number. As soon as the phone is answered you will hear the volunteer say something like:

'Hello this is Samaritans can I help you.'

As soon as you get the opportunity you will be able to speak generally with the volunteer. At some point in the conversation the volunteer will probably ask if you are suicidal. This opens up the opportunity for you to share. At this point you might say something like:

"I am actually feeling suicidal. I want to let go of this feeling."

The volunteer may encourage you to continue sharing and talking about it. This is good! The more you share with the right people the better you will feel. When the call ends say to yourself:

"I now let go of this suicidal feeling. I am safe and secure at all times and under all conditions." Repeat!

You will notice there are no frills on these sentences they are short, specific and to the point. Obviously, this would be a very mechanical way to have a conversation and in an actual call you might say things differently, but the message stays the same. After sharing you will begin to feel relief almost immediately it may take you a bit of time to get used to the idea that you are feeling better. So, be patient with yourself.

The examples are given as a guide but you can follow them literally if you need to. Experience has shown that the quickest way to let thoughts and feelings go is to be as specific as possible. When you are more familiar with using the steps, your sharing will become less mechanical.

When the sentences used in the sharing above are set out alongside the steps they look like:

Name it: *I am feeling suicidal. I now let go of this feeling.*
Share it: *I am feeling suicidal. I now let go of this feeling.*
Replace it: *I am safe and secure at all times. Repeat!*

A Suicidal Thought
Thinking about suicide and feeling suicidal are very different. It can occur in many ways during the course of any given day for example, you may overhear someone having a conversation about it, you may come across the topic in a news bulletin or newspaper article. It is virtually impossible to avoid the subject of suicide these days.

How or why these thoughts come is not all that important. What is important is that you are able to deal with them when they do come. You can deal with a thought of suicide in exactly the same way as you did with the feeling. If using the helpline share as follows:

I am thinking about suicide. I now let go of this thought. I am safe and secure at all times.

As with the previous example when these sentences are set out alongside the steps they will look as follows:

Name it: *I am thinking about suicide. I now let go of this thought.*
Share it: *I am thinking about suicide. I now let go of this thought.*

Replace it: *I am safe, secure and clear headed at all times. Repeat!*

When dealing with thoughts and feelings around self-harm it is absolutely essential you have someone to share with. If you do not have someone to share with it is strongly recommended that you ring or contact one of the helplines.

As mentioned, Samaritans are trained to listen to callers who are sharing their thoughts and feelings around suicide and they can be contacted from anywhere in the world through e-mail. This is an anonymous service. Remember there are helplines all over the world so you will not be stuck for someone to share with wherever you are.

They Come and Go

Thoughts and feelings come and then they go if you let them but, you have to know how to let them. Being able to name share and replace them will bring great peace and happiness into your life! All thoughts and feelings can be replaced using the steps. The kinds of thoughts and feelings being dealt with in these paragraphs are among the most difficult human beings have to deal with. When you have learned to deal with these everything else will be so simple.

Sharing should be carried out as soon as possible after naming the feeling, attitude, thought or emotion with which you are dealing. It has the effect of shrinking the thought or feeling before letting it go completely.

Other Ways to Share

Along with sharing thoughts and feelings by phone, one to one or in groups you can also share by e-Mail or text. For simplicity, the Samaritans will be used again to illustrate the use of e-mail or texting. The e-mail address is **jo@samaritans.ie** If you decide to use e-mail sharing, make sure to share the exact thoughts and feelings you want to deal with. Keep your sharing specific for best results.

Sample e-Mail Sharing

Hi Jo,

I am e-mailing to share a troublesome thought with you. I am thinking about suicide today. I am sharing this thought to let it go.

Thank you for being there! John

Or you might write something like:

Hi Jo,

I am e-mailing to share a feeling that's troubling me today. I'm feeling suicidal. I am sharing this feeling so that I can let it go.

Thank you, Mary

Use Specific Language

These e-mails are just two simple examples of how you might begin sharing with Samaritans. In these examples you are sharing thoughts and feelings around self-harm and suicide. You can also share about other life situations by e-mail. As with all sharing it is essential when using e-mail to state exactly what's bothering you.

When you have the exact problem shared in this way you can always explore it further in a future e-mail or communication if you wish. The important thing is to keep your e-mail specific. If your sharing is vague you will end up holding on to most of the problem. So, share the thought or feeling exactly and your purpose will be achieved.

Use the Steps as Your Guide

The examples above are given as a guide to illustrate the importance of sharing "specifically" when you are practising the first two steps. Remember, you must name and then share exactly what it is you want to let go of otherwise it will not happen. This is essential especially when sharing thoughts and feelings around self-harm and suicide.

The more you practise the easier it becomes. Keep in mind, you may have to name and share a thought or feeling a few times before you can let it go fully. Stick with it, use the steps as your guide and you will be able to let go of all your troublesome thoughts and feelings no matter what they are.

Additional Thoughts on Sharing

As you can see, sharing can be done through all or any of the following: spoken, written, typed, video, phone calls, sign language. Whatever way you decide to share, it is essential that you have total confidence in the person with whom you are sharing. This person does not need to have any special qualifications but they do need to be trustworthy, kind and compassionate. It is also important that they know exactly what you are doing.

The ability to be able to listen without giving advice is a quality that's also desirable. Remember too you are not looking for a counselling session or to have a conversation about what you are sharing. Advice or other comments are not necessary for you to get the benefit of sharing in fact, advice is not recommended at all unless it is given by a professional.

Protect Your Privacy
Part of the letting go process can be to write your troublesome thoughts and feelings down. They can

then be let go by sharing and destroying the paper immediately. Burning the paper and watching it go up in smoke is actually a very symbolic way of letting go.

If you write something private on a piece of paper, burn or destroy it in some way as soon as possible after you share. It can be very therapeutic to get your thoughts and feelings out of your head and on to a piece of paper but do not leave them lying around.

If You Can't Find Someone to Share With

If, for some reason, you can't find someone you trust to share with and you do not want to contact a helpline, you can practise the steps on your own for a while. Although this is only a temporary measure it will give some relief but it will not be permanent. In this situation, you can practise the steps as they are set out here:

> **Name it**: *I am thinking about suicide. I am now letting go of this thought.*
> **Share it**: *I am thinking about suicide. I am now letting go of this thought. I will share it when the opportunity arises.*
> **Replace it**: *I am safe and secure at all times.* Repeat!

Doing the steps in this way will ensure that your progress is not hindered while you continue to search for someone to share with. This will work so long as you are sincere and willing to share when the opportunity arises.

Just like the three steps are the core of this whole approach to greater well-being, "sharing" is the core of the three steps. If you want to have lasting peace and happiness step two, in its entirety, is essential. Sharing is the corner stone of the three core steps and the foundation for building real fellowship.

Fellowship

In the long term, it will be important that you have close fellowship with at least one other human being. Therefore, the sooner you find someone to share with, the better. However, this does not mean you should rush it.

One of the outcomes of sharing with a person you choose is that a particular kind of bond will develop between you. These relationships are based on kindness, compassion, trustworthiness and the ability to listen; altogether, this amounts to unconditional love. Once formed these relationships will last and cannot be separated by distance or time.

In the Meantime

Until you find someone to share with helplines and other voluntary groups are available, along with professional councillors, therapists, life coaches and psychologists. Do not hesitate to call or contact Samaritans or a similar helpline especially if you are troubled in any way about suicide.

These helplines cannot be recommended highly enough. There are also anonymous self-help groups available, where you can share and have fellowship. Most self-help groups operate unconditionally and the only thing you need to join is to be willing to try and improve your life.

The Vacuum

After you have practised step two you will start to feel the benefits but it is important that you do not stop at this point. Certainly, you will be starting to change and you may even think it is enough. However, experience has shown that if you stop after steps one and two, the benefit will not be permanent.

Generally speaking, after you practise steps one and two, you will experience a period of calm. Unfortunately, this will not last. This is just like being in the eye of a storm. This calm will act like a vacuum and start to suck in other troublesome thoughts and feelings and soon, you will find yourself right back where you started.

If you want the benefit of steps one and two to last you must start practising step three immediately. This will fill the vacuum with thoughts and feelings that promote lasting happiness, peace of mind and well-being.

Strange and Awkward

You are well on your way at this stage. However, if all this feels odd and uncomfortable to you right now, it is because that is the way it is supposed to be. Just like when you are learning and trying to practise anything new: it will feel strange and awkward at first. As you become more familiar with the steps and go deeper into how they work, practice will become much easier and even enjoyable. Stick with it and you will see a whole new world open up before you. The signs of this new world start to emerge the minute you start to practise step one sincerely. If you keep going and become consistent in your practice, you will awaken to a new existence.

CHAPTER TEN

Step Three – a bit deeper

Replace It

Just like the first two steps, step three is easy to learn and simple to use. As you grow and develop, you will need to increase your understanding of what you are doing. Otherwise, your progress will be very limited. That's why you need to know what is happening and what needs to happen when you replace troublesome thoughts and feelings. It is why you need these deeper discussions on the steps.

The purpose of step three is to replace the troublesome thoughts and feelings that you named and shared in steps one and two. This is not some kind of partial clear out of emotional liabilities. With practice, it will be the complete replacement of feelings, attitudes, thoughts and emotions, troublesome or otherwise. During the practice of step three, these will be replaced by human qualities, such as kindness, compassion, joy, peace, happiness and contentment.

You may be thinking, how can this be done? This is a step too far! If you have been practising steps one and two, you have the hard work done! If you haven't worked on the other two steps yet, start now. It will literally take just a few seconds to get started.

The complete replacement of thoughts and feelings is achieved by first practising the three steps. Then developing your awareness of what you are actually doing, why you do it and who benefits. These are the first two principles of mastery mentioned in Chapter 3. If you do not know who benefits or why you do what you do any success you have will be temporary and of no lasting value to anyone.

When you are practising step three you will be replacing your old feelings, attitudes, thoughts and emotions completely. You will not be reinstating or laundering any of them. All your old thoughts and feelings have to go completely. This is done by practising steps one and two and then replacing them completely in step three. To help you with this clear out of the old you can make use of the emotional inventory in Chapter 6.

Underlying Working Parts

Generally speaking thoughts and feelings come and go if you let them. When you practise the three steps, you will be advancing the natural flow of your thoughts and feelings. Replacing old thoughts and feelings is a crucial part of this coming and going because you are actively putting the kind of healthy feelings, attitudes, thoughts and emotions you need back into your life.

As with the other two steps, there are also many underlying working parts in step three. These are switched on when you begin to apply the step. Three of these are now explored:

Substitution
Affirmation
Consolidation

Substitution

No doubt, you are familiar with the term substitute. It is simply another name for replacing one thing with another. In this case, you are going to substitute one feeling or thought for another. For example, a feeling of hate can be substituted by a feeling of love; an attitude of prejudice can be substituted by an attitude of tolerance; a thought of violence can be substituted by a thought of peace; an emotional outburst can be substituted by a feeling of calm.

This kind of substitution is one of the underlying features activated as a result of practising the third step. Substitution is necessary because certain kinds of thoughts and feelings do not mix well together. For example, a person who is filled with hate is incapable of love; a person filled with prejudice is incapable of tolerance. One will eventually dominate the other: which one depends on which one is practised most.

At some stage in your life, you may have heard someone say or maybe you have even said it yourself, "I hate this" or "I hate that". This kind of thinking and self-talk has to be removed and substituted. Consider, when you practise step one and two, you are naming and sharing these kinds of thoughts and feelings. When you are practising step three the substitution of this kind of thinking takes place for example, "I hate this…" is substituted with "I love this…".

In the context of step three this is a temporary replacement. The substitution still needs to be affirmed and consolidated before the thought or feeling is replaced completely. This is because there will be a period of back and forth between the old thought or feeling and the new.

Substitution and Attitude

Attitudes, like thoughts, feelings and emotions, have also to be substituted and then replaced completely. Destructive attitudes, such as prejudice and intolerance, are the kind of traits that will completely destroy your life and take any trace of happiness and peace of mind you have. They are the seeds of discrimination, bigotry and racism therefore, they have to be replaced. After naming and sharing prejudice and intolerance, they can be substituted with an attitude of patience and tolerance and then permanently replaced by these qualities.

Some attitudes can be very dangerous and disturbing. They can remain hidden until some life event exposes them. For example, racial intolerance can remain hidden for years, only to be exposed in life situations such as cross-cultural encounters, political speeches, leadership styles and attitude, to mention a few. Attitudes can be very destructive.

Thoughts and Substitution

Your thinking is absolutely critical to your mental, physical and spiritual well-being. Therefore, it is crucial that you cultivate healthy thinking. Your thinking is really at the interface between you and the world around you. How you think and what you think feeds the way you perceive the world you inhabit.

Most thoughts come and go. They are like the waves of the ocean that break upon the shoreline. However, some of these thoughts stick around. This is not a problem if the thoughts that stay around are healthy thoughts. The difficulty starts when your thinking is hijacked by thoughts that bring fear and anxiety into your life. These thoughts need to be substituted and replaced as quickly as possible. For example, a thought of hostility can be substituted with a thought of tranquillity.

Emotions and Substitution

Emotions are managed in exactly the same way as feelings, attitudes and thoughts: by applying the three steps. To do this effectively you need to know the difference between them. It is particularly easy to get mixed up between emotions and feelings. This is probably because people have been educated into seeing feelings as either positive or negative emotions. This is generally held to be true in the many schools of thought in the fields of psychology. However, that is only one way of looking at feelings and emotions.

You can also look at emotions and feelings as having separate identities. The simplest way to understand this concept is to view feelings as long term and emotions as short term. For example, the love of a mother will last a lifetime and is therefore long term. On the other hand, an emotional response is generally short term and may last just a few seconds but can be very intense. For example, an emotional outburst or panic attack.

Emotional Outbursts

Emotional outbursts are very difficult to deal with when they are happening in real time. In this sense, they are a bit like panic attacks, in that if you are having a panic attack, it can be very difficult to return to a state of calm.

Panic is not too far removed from hysteria. This is because of the intensity involved in these responses to certain life events. The question is, how do you manage panic, hysteria and emotional outbursts? The short answer is, prevention.

The approach in this book is designed to help you move to a level of being where you are able to manage your emotional responses to life. For some people this will happen quickly and for some it will not be as fast. Until it happens and you are fully confident you are able to handle situations that bring on intense responses it is best to avoid them. This means avoiding the situations that bring on emotional outbursts, hysteria or panic as much as possible.

This is a good tactic, especially when you are just beginning to practise the three steps and the other suggestions. Obviously, you will not be able to use this tactic all the time but it can be useful in the early stages of your journey.

Over time, as you become more familiar with the steps and the other suggestions, you will be better equipped to tackle the situations that cause extreme anxiety and panic. In the meantime, be patient and do what you can do. Soon, you will find that you are able to manage all the tests and challenges that life throws at you. The chapter on meditation, mindfulness and awareness (see Chapter 14) will also help you deal with whatever life throws at you.

Affirmation

Affirmation is another essential underlying working part of the third step and needs a deeper exploration. It amounts to affirming to yourself that the old ideas have been replaced with the new. However, replacing troublesome feelings attitudes, thoughts and emotions requires the targeted use of affirmations. Therefore affirmations are central to the whole idea of replacing. They are not a new concept; they have their origin in the distant past. However, the way in which they are used in today's world is relatively new. Some of the earliest records of affirmations come from the Bible and other ancient and later Scriptures. All affirmations are inspired by and have their foundation in the wisdom of the past and the hope of the future.

Nothing Original

Except for a few instances, direct quotations, from any source, have not been used in this text to avoid turning it into an academic exercise. On the other hand the ideas and principles set out in these pages are obviously inspired by the wisdom of the past and life experiences.

Therefore, the affirmations used are not by any stretch of the imagination original. Similar ones can be found in most self-help books. Be that as it is, affirmations are powerful yet very simple tools to have at your disposal. They can be used anywhere at any time. They become even more powerful when used in conjunction with an approach to well-being, such as the approach in these pages.

Affirmations a Definition

For the purpose of this book affirmations are defined as, *well-chosen words, carefully put together in the present tense, for the purpose of intentionally replacing troublesome feelings, attitudes, thoughts and emotions*. They can be repeated as often as you want to inspire change and promote well-being. Remember the words you use in your daily life have a profound effect on how you think and feel about yourself and the people you associate with. In fact the words you use will influence and have an effect on every aspect of your life.

Words are Powerful Energy

The words you use are a powerful energy. They can build you up or knock you down. This energy is, in a sense, vibrating at a frequency. Used in affirmations, words can be seen as being charged with a higher frequency and their power is multiplied. Similar to what happens with the words of a song, they have the power to create emotional and spiritual responses in the listener. In well-constructed affirmations, they will do exactly the same thing, they are a powerful energy and have amazing influence. They can make you laugh and cry and they will heal you if used correctly.

The correct use of words in affirmations will have a healing effect on your mental, physical and spiritual health. They are powerful in their effect and will, if applied correctly, have a profound impact on your whole being. The following is an example of an affirmation:

I am calm and relaxed under all conditions.

Although, in this book affirmations are considered more effective when used as part of the three steps, it is important to be aware that they can also be used to good effect as a standalone exercise. In fact, they are often used in this way. To use them as a standalone exercise, say and repeat the affirmation often, pausing after each repetition for a couple of seconds to let it sink in. For example say and repeat:

I am calm and relaxed under all conditions. Pause for a couple of seconds. Repeat often!

Caution!

Despite the fact that this is a good practice to develop keep in mind that affirmations work best after old thoughts and feelings are named, shared and removed as in steps one and two. This is particularly important when dealing with very troublesome thoughts and feelings. Remember this!

With and Without Steps

When using affirmations without the steps most if not all of the time you will be saying you feel a certain way before you do. For example, when you use the following affirmation, you will probably be saying, "I am calm under all conditions" before you are. This is what occurs when you use affirmations on their own. Again this is simply because you will be affirming something before it has happened and although using affirmations in this way works it will take longer for the new feeling to take hold because you will be mixing the old with the new.

On the other hand when using affirmations with the three steps they will work much more effectively. This is because you will already have let go of the old thoughts and feelings in steps one and two and will be replacing them in step three. That is, you will already have let go of the old troublesome feelings, attitudes, thoughts and emotions before you begin affirming their replacement with an affirmation.

Creating Affirmations

It is always good idea to create and use your own affirmations. When doing so, keep in mind that you do not have to reinvent the wheel. In other words, you do not have to be original. However affirmations do have to be written in the present tense and they have to be specific.

If you are completely new to the concept of affirmations you will need some help to begin creating your own. Consider the following words: calm, accept, peace, composure. Let's say these are qualities you want to have in your life. To create affirmations using these words start the first one with the words "I am…":

Calm: I am calm under all conditions.
Accept: I accept the gift of life.
Peace: I have peace in my life at all times.
Composure: I am composed in every situation.

Using the words "I am" will help keep you in the present tense when creating your affirmations. So too will "I accept…" and "I have…".

You will notice too that the affirmations are very simple and similar to one another. You may even have seen or heard them before. That's okay, this is not an exercise in creative writing. The goal is to put affirmations together that work best for you.

Writing and Speaking Affirmations

Affirmations, they can be written and spoken and then acted on. By "written" is meant writing an affirmation by hand a number of times. For example write:

I have peace in my life at all times. Pause and repeat!

By spoken is meant they can be said aloud or quietly to yourself for example say aloud or to yourself:

I am loved. Pause and repeat!

There are no specific rules on how to do this or, the number of times that you write an affirmation. Try writing an affirmation three times and saying it three times as a standalone exercise. Don't forget to pause between repetitions when you are speaking them. By the way, saying an affirmation even once is beneficial but you will need much more than that to get full and permanent benefit.

Just a Few Seconds

Although the above-mentioned affirmations are very simple, they are also very powerful. Practise them as with all the other affirmations in this book until, like the three steps, they are a spontaneous response to troublesome thoughts and feelings. Use them along with the affirmations you create yourself to give you that extra boost. Remember just a few seconds of practice, a few times throughout the day will work wonders for you. Yes! A few seconds of practice is all it takes. Write them down. Say them. Write them out again. Say them again. Repeat often. You can't practise too much. Practise until you feel the change then keep going.

Self-Respect

The words that you use, from now on, take on a whole new meaning because you now know how important they are to your well-being. Your words are now part of the foundation of the new you. Affirmation requires the frequent use of words that will always reflect your attitude towards yourself.

To explore this a bit further, ask yourself, what would happen if you repeatedly told a person whom you had complete control over – let's say, a child – that they are useless and good for nothing? Soon, they would start to accept this as being true. The same thing happens if you treat yourself in this way. You will eventually feel useless and good for nothing. This is a simple example but highlights the need to be aware of the language you use on yourself and others.

Remember, your words have the power to influence and even control your feelings, attitude, thoughts and emotions. Therefore, the language you use towards yourself must always be uplifting, encouraging and loving. You must treat yourself with self-respect at all times. This attitude towards yourself is one of the indicators of wellness. The respect you have for yourself will be evident in all of your relationships because if you do not respect yourself, you will not respect anyone else.

Getting the Most from Affirmations

In the context of step three, an affirmation is a statement that is repeated often, affirming that a troublesome thought or feeling has been replaced. As was mentioned earlier saying and repeating a relevant affirmation immediately after doing steps one and two will have a more powerful effect than doing the affirmations alone. Therefore the three steps should always be applied as a unit for best results. An example will illustrate this point.

Let's say you have a resentment towards a colleague who was promoted ahead of you at work. The steps can be applied as follows:

Name it: I resent my work colleague, John Doe because he was promoted ahead of me. I now let go of this resentment.

Share it: I resent my work colleague, John Doe because he was promoted ahead of me. I now let go of this resentment.

Replace it: I wish John Doe well in his new position. I love my own position at work and my promotion is on the way.

Once You are Willing

The affirmation, *I wish John well in his new position* is simple to say in that it is not complicated. However, it may be difficult to say because, at the time you are saying it, you may not feel like wishing John well. This will depend on how deep-rooted the resentment is. If this happens to you, try writing the affirmation down first before saying it. A bit of perseverance during these times will keep you on track. You can always repeat the first two steps again and pay particular attention when you are sharing the resentment.

Once you are willing, you will succeed in replacing the resentment and with practice, you will get used to applying affirmations to almost every situation. The benefits of using affirmations will be amazing if you practise them with the three steps. Affirmations and their practical use will be explored further in the next chapter they are being discussed here as an essential part of the third step.

About Resentment

Resentments can be very tough to deal with. When you start to practise this step, you may find it difficult to even think these kinds of affirmations, let alone say or write them down. This, of course, depends on how deep-rooted the resentment is.

No matter how difficult the affirmation is to say, the rewards will far outweigh the discomfort of saying them. Persevere and you will experience what it is like to be emotionally free. Resentment is a taker. It is nasty and poisonous. It can and will remove any trace of happiness from your life.

It is easier to let go of a resentment before it takes hold because, the longer you leave it, the more of a grip it will get and the more damage it will do. So, if you have any resentments in your life, let them go. The reason why you have to let go of resentments is so that you will have peace of mind. This is not about trying to make anyone else feel better; it is all about making you feel better.

Consolidation

After you have let go of your troublesome thoughts and feelings in steps one and two, your mind will be left with empty space and will behave like a vacuum. Therefore this space needs to be filled immediately but the filling cannot be more of the same: otherwise, you will be right back where you started. Therefore, the old thoughts and feelings have to be replaced with new qualities, for example kindness and compassion. These are the kinds of qualities that bring happiness and contentment into your life and cultivates the kind of disposition your life will project.

You will of course want the action of replacing your troublesome thoughts and feelings to be permanent. This means your newfound happiness and peace of mind needs to be consolidated. The correct practice of replacing troublesome thoughts and feelings will have the effect of consolidating your newfound happiness with a deepening sense of well-being.

An Exercise in Consolidation

You will need a pen and paper to complete this consolidation exercise. Let's say, as in the example mentioned earlier in this chapter, you are still having difficulty dealing with the resentment against John Doe because of the promotion he got at work. First, practise steps one and two. Next, over a period of twenty-one days, write the following replacing affirmation twenty-one times each day in one sitting:

Replace it: I wish John Doe well in his new position. I love my own position at work and my promotion is on the way.

Twenty-one is the magic number in this exercise: outside of the fact that you get the key to the door when you are twenty-one, the experts say it takes twenty-one days to break a habit. Some experts take this further and say it takes ninety days for a new habit to become a way of life. Therefore, to be sure that the resentment does not come back into your life, continue the practice for ninety days to ensure consolidation.

Right now, you may think this exercise is a bit extreme. However, keep in mind that resentment, even the smallest one, can do real damage to you and your loved ones. It can lead to serious mental and physical illness and needs to be removed from your life. Otherwise, it will leave you and anyone close to you miserable. Therefore, it really is worth doing this exercise.

You will not have to do this exercise all the time but this is an option especially if you are dealing with something really troublesome. You can also use this exercise if there is a particular quality you would really love to have in your life. For example if you want to be, calm and relaxed at all times use the following affirmation in this consolidation exercise:

Replace it: I am calm and relaxed at all times and under all conditions.

Write it down twenty-one times a day for ninety days. Writing affirmations is a great habit to cultivate every day if you can. So too is saying and repeating affirmations.

A Solid Foundation

If you are willing to practise replacing and the other two steps sincerely, you will already have a solid foundation for your well-being in place. This is because willingness is another one of the essential ingredients for your success. If you have willingness, you are already well on your way to transforming your life for good.

This book and these deeper discussions are ultimately a sharing of ideas and suggestions to help increase your understanding and awareness of how simple it is to have real happiness and contentment in your life permanently. After going through the quick guide, you know you have to practise the three steps to let go of troublesome thoughts and feelings. This is absolutely essential if you ever want peace of mind and happiness in your life. The steps alone will get you well on your way but reading about what you have to do will not be enough you will have to do it!

Don't just Read It; Do It

The difficulty in this approach is not in knowing what you have to do but, in actually doing what you now know. Many people read a book like this one on how to do something. They go to the seminar, do the course, fill their head with information but never apply what they have learned. They are just collectors of information and end up worse than they were before. The books become what has been described as "shelf help" by those in the know. It is a waste of time to be an information collector. Information is useless unless you use it.

Once you know how to practise a few of the suggestion in this book, you are on the road and although there are many suggestions to help you along, the fact remains that it takes only seconds to apply the three steps and the other suggestions in this book. The meditations can also be shortened and lengthened as required.

When? Why?
When and why do you replace thoughts and feelings? Ideally all thoughts and feelings should be replaced each day. The three steps are used to do this quickly. All feelings, attitudes, thoughts and emotions should be replaced as soon as they are shared in step two. The question as to why is equally as simple to answer. This is because, if you do not replace them and replace them immediately, you will quickly attract even more troublesome thoughts and feelings into your life. So, everyday name, share and replace them.

There is no halfway house when it comes to practising these steps. You cannot half do them: it is all or nothing. The simple answers to when and why you replace troublesome thoughts and feelings:

When? Immediately after sharing.
Why? The old thoughts will come back if you don't.

Recap: A Few Important Points

The three steps are a process in themselves and need to be practised together. If you practise steps one and two and ignore the third step, troublesome thoughts and feelings will return and the likelihood is they will bring some friends and relatives with them.

Your happiness and well-being depend on practising the three steps together. Therefore, along with naming and sharing troublesome thoughts and feelings they must be replaced immediately. Otherwise all you will be doing is creating a vacuum that sucks in other troublesome thoughts and feelings.

The whole purpose of steps one and two is to catch and let go of troublesome thoughts and feelings. The purpose of step three is to replace thoughts and feelings after you have let them go so that they can't comeback. Of the three steps "naming" is the brain, "sharing" is the heart, "replacing" is the spirit. Use them together!

The Power of Words

The words you use have an enormous effect on your being. Words put together in the form of affirmations and repeated often with intent can soften the hardest of hearts and have a powerful healing effect on the speaker and the listener. Words can make you laugh or cry, miserable or happy, tolerant or intolerant, kind and compassionate. Your words affect every part of your life.

Be Careful in Your Choice of Words

Now that you are more aware of the power of the words you use, you must be careful in your choices. This awareness will help you use language that will not sabotage your efforts. Furthermore although the words you use in your day-to-day life have a powerful effect on you and those around you the words you use in affirmations are even more powerful. They affect every part of your being. They also affect everyone who hears them. It follows then, that when you practise affirmations to replace troublesome thoughts and feelings, it is essential to get it right. Therefore, in the interest of your greater well-being, choose your words wisely.

I'm Not Able; I Can't!

Human beings can spend a lot of their precious time looking at what is wrong in their lives; what they haven't got or what they can't do. As a result of this attitude, their affirmations and self-talk include statements like, "I can't do it", "I'm not able", "It's hard for me". These are examples of words chosen badly. If you talk like this to yourself often enough, it will eventually stick.

These statements are very unhelpful and do untold damage. How affected by it you are depends on how much of it you have subjected yourself to. This kind of self-demeaning attitude is of no benefit to you or anyone else whatsoever. It will serve only to keep you in the grip of negativity. If you have been mistreating or belittling yourself in this way, the time has come to stop. Say, "I can do it" instead of "I can't do it". "I am able to" instead of "I am not able". "It's easy for me" instead of "It's hard for me".

Say: *I can do it. I am able to. It's easy for me.* Repeat!

All Negative Self-Talk Must Stop

The affirmations you create yourself and the ones used in this text are essential when replacing negative self-talk and troublesome thoughts and feelings. Negative and belittling self-talk must be avoided at all times. For example, calling yourself "stupid" or "foolish" is a complete no-no. For best results, the affirmations for replacing negative self-talk should be used along with the three steps. Refusing to allow any negative self-talk into your life is now of primary importance and will advance your overall well-being immeasurably.

Traits and Qualities

One way to get a better understanding of the different kinds of thoughts and feelings is to see them as traits and qualities. For example, jealousy, resentments and intolerance can be seen as human traits. On the other hand, kindness, compassion, tolerance can be seen as human qualities. During the practice of the third step, you can see yourself as replacing human traits with human qualities.

For example, the feeling or human trait of jealousy can be replaced by the feeling or human quality of admiration. The attitude or human trait of intolerance can be replaced by an attitude or human quality of patience. A thought of, or human trait of violence can be replaced by the human quality of peace. The human traits of emotional outbursts can be replaced by the human quality of composure.

In this way, human traits are removed and replaced by human qualities, using affirmations. One more example will show the three steps in action again, this time dealing with the human trait of jealousy. Let's say you are feeling jealous of your neighbour because they have just bought a new car:

> **Name it**: I feel jealous of my neighbour because they bought a new car. I now let go of this feeling.
> **Share it**: I feel jealous of my neighbour because they have a new car. I now let go of this feeling.
> **Replace it**: I wish my neighbour well. I love their new car.

The Switches

Every exercise in this chapter takes only seconds to apply. It takes daily practice to be able to apply them spontaneously to the unexpected events a day may bring. Along with the three steps the exercises are designed so that they can be practised while you are at work, at play or at rest.

They can be used like switches. For example, if you are in a locked room with no source of light other than a light which is operated by a switch, you will have to use the switch if you want light. Being willing and able to use the switch is absolutely essential otherwise you will remain in the dark. You will also need to know where the switch is because remember, the room is dark.

There are switches in this book in the form of the three steps and additional suggestions. These switches will turn on the light of peace and contentment for you in your life if you use them. On the other hand, if you do not use the switches, you will have no peace and contentment!

How Long Will It Take?
The question is often asked, how long will it take to break the old thought patterns and replace them permanently with the new? A time frame of twenty-one days to break an old habit and ninety days to consolidate the new behaviour was mentioned earlier.

These suggested time frames have their merit but there are many more. There are those who will tell you it takes seven days, some will say twenty-one days, yet others will tell you, more than sixty days to break a habit.

More than likely, the real answer to this question is that it depends on how willing you are to let go of the old thoughts and feelings. The transformation can and does happen instantly for those who want it more than anything else and are willing to do whatever it takes. For others it will take a little longer.

Instant Benefit
In general, acquiring lasting happiness, peace of mind, and a greater sense of well-being is a gradual process.

Nevertheless, you will start to feel better from the moment you begin to practise the three steps sincerely. Beyond that if you are willing to continue you will make progress rapidly. In sum from the moment you take your first steps you will feel benefit and this will continue for as long as you are willing to change.

Motivators or Tormentors

If you are a long way away from where you want to be, then you will have a great motivator because you will be feeling the pain of loneliness, isolation and probably despair among other tormentors. Remember, pain is a great motivator. In fact, there are those who say, "no pain no gain."

Some would even say that pain is a gift, yet the moment a pain is felt, it's time to complain. Usually, pain is a warning that something is wrong and needs to be addressed. It does not matter if the pain is mental, physical or emotional it will drive you on to find a solution if you listen to it.

If the pain is bad enough, it will remove most of the resistance to change. This means that you will be more willing to do whatever it takes to let go of the pain of intolerable, troublesome thoughts and feelings and embrace the happiness and peace of the new life that awaits you. Unfortunately, some people have a very high tolerance for pain and will suffer greatly before taking action.

Coming and Going

It is impossible to replace feelings attitudes, thoughts and emotions unless you first remove the old ones. This is why it is necessary to practise the three steps as a progression going from step one to two and then to three. They will not work in any other way. The steps work as a unit and the starting point is step one. After practising the steps for a while, you will be able to calmly observe your thoughts and feelings flow through your mind and they will no longer concern you.

The Natural Flow

There is a natural flow to thoughts and feelings as mentioned earlier, they come and then they go if you let them. Some thoughts and feelings appear to be stickier than others and seem reluctant to leave. However, work the steps and share them as often as you can and even the stickiest thoughts and feelings will lose their grip.

The point is that you are going to have thoughts and feelings but they will now follow the natural flow. In other words, they will come and go because you will let them.

Chapter Eleven

More About Affirmations

Affirmations, in one form or another, have been used by all living creatures since the beginning of time. A dog will constantly bark and behave in a particular way to affirm its authority or lack of it and of course, cats are experts at letting you know who's the boss and will constantly affirm their status. I dare say, even plants use affirmations but we won't go there! However since human beings are able to talk, use words and in some ways have a more refined level of consciousness, affirmations can be used to greater effect.

By now the importance of affirmations and the words you use is well established. In this chapter you will see how affirmations can transform your life when used correctly. First you will be reminded again of what affirmations are. Then you will be introduced to some of the different kinds of affirmation you may come across. Their intentional and unintentional use will also be mentioned before you are introduced to one of the most famous and successful examples of affirmations in action.

What are Affirmations?

Affirmations have already been defined in the previous chapter as "well-chosen words, carefully put together, in the present tense, for the purpose of intentionally replacing troublesome feelings, attitudes, thoughts and emotions." This definition has been created for the purpose of this book which is basically a guide to peace of mind and contentment. The more you know about affirmations the more you will realise how important they are to your overall well-being.

Intentional and Unintentional

Affirmations are used, sometimes unintentionally and sometimes intentionally. Intentional use of affirmations is when you say exactly what you mean and intend, for example "I am a worthwhile human being". On the other hand unintentional use of affirmations is when you say something you may not really mean or intend such as, "I'm not good enough". The unintentional use of affirmations must be avoided.

An affirmation can be just one word. For example, maybe there were times when you said "yes" when you wished you said "no". Another example you've probably heard people use is "I can't believe it" Some people unintentionally say this when something really good happens for them. They say the opposite of what they mean. This can have the effect of nullifying their good fortune.

The point is you need to avoid unintentional use of words on their own or as affirmations because this kind of self-talk will slow your progress down or may even stop your progress altogether. If you become aware that you are using unintentional affirmations change it immediately. This will mean changing "I can't believe it" into "I do believe it". You can also change your unintentional "yes" or "no" into an intentional "yes" or an intentional "no".

Human beings are creatures of habit and as affirmations are habit-forming, when you practise using them intentionally, they will quickly become a habit. As your awareness of what you are actually doing grows, you are less likely to use unintended affirmations. If you are in the habit of using unintended words or affirmations on yourself, the time has come to change. This kind of negative unintended self-talk will slow down or may even stop your progress towards well-being altogether.

Unhelpful to Helpful

Intended affirmations are used specifically to promote your well-being and therefore are designed to be helpful. On the other hand unintended affirmations are not helpful and will be very damaging to your well-being. It is very important to be able to differentiate between the two. Remember the words you use have a powerful effect on you and all who hear them. Being aware of this will help prevent you from using them. This will remove a major obstacle to your progress.

One other thing. Let's say someone is using unhelpful and unsupportive affirmations to you, for example, telling you on a regular basis that "you'll never be any good". This is just as bad or even worse than saying it yourself. Tell them to stop. If you can't confront the situation in this way, try to keep your distance from this person until you can deal with the situation. This, by the way, as you are probably aware, is a form of bullying.

When you are turning your own unhelpful affirmations around start by saying "I can" instead of "I can't". You can turn any unhelpful affirmations around in this way. These examples are very simple but serve the purpose perfectly.

Patience

You will need to be patient with yourself and others as you begin to make these changes. To practise patience use the three steps. You can work out the wording for the first two steps then use the following affirmation for step three:

Replace it: I am patient with myself and others at all times. Repeat!

Remember to pause for a few seconds between repetitions!

Functions of Affirmations

Affirmations can be applied in many ways and can have different functions. For example, they can be spoken, shouted, whispered, sung and written. By definition affirmations are intended to function as a means to promote your well-being and improve your life. In the context of the three steps their function is to replace troublesome feelings, attitudes, thoughts and emotions. These are replaced with lasting peace of mind, contentment, kindness, and compassion, resulting in your whole life being transformed.

In step one, if you are dealing with fear, you will name it as follows, "I am afraid of being alone". Although this statement is worded similar to an affirmation it is not functioning as an affirmation. It is functioning as an admission and an acknowledgement of something. If this wording were being used as an affirmation, it would be very unhelpful. This is why it is immediately followed by "I now let go of this fear".

When you practise step one these two statements are brought together as one statement as follows: "I am afraid of being alone. I now let go of this fear." The same wording is then used when practising step two to ensure you share exactly what the fear is. Step three is then used to replace the fear and is straight forward in so far as its function is to replace troublesome thoughts and feelings.

In the practice of step one, remember you are not affirming what's wrong. You are acknowledging, admitting and identifying a fear or whatever is wrong for the purpose of letting it go. This is a very important distinction and needs to be understood. That is why when you are new to the practise of the steps, you should stick to the script and practise them exactly as they are written. Remember, the wording of steps one and two are identical for example:

> **Name it**: I am feeling sad. I am now letting go of this feeling.
> **Share it**: I am feeling sad. I am now letting go of this feeling.
> **Replace it**: I am happy and contented at all times. Repeat!

Not every feeling, attitude, thought or emotion will be as clear cut as this example.

Do Affirmations Work?

One of the most famous and public uses of affirmations is by a boxer by the name of Cassius Clay, later known as Muhammad Ali.

Cassius Clay

It was mentioned earlier that affirmations are a form of powerful self-talk and can affect everyone who hears them and if used correctly they will have an enormous effect on how you feel and act.

A very public master class was given by one of the most famous users of affirmations in the twentieth century. He was a young man by the name of Cassius Clay. He was a boxer from the United States of America and won a gold medal in the 1960 Olympics in Rome, at the age of 18.

Muhammad Ali

The Olympic Gold Medal was just the start for Cassius Clay, who changed his name to Muhammad Ali in

1964, after defeating Sonny Liston to become the world heavyweight boxing champion. One of his most famous affirmations was, *I am the greatest*. He is quoted as saying, "I am the greatest. I said that even before I knew I was."

In other words, he was saying that he was the greatest before he was, and knew he was. Remember this because it is exactly what you will be doing when you are applying affirmations. You will be saying and affirming you are "happy and contented" before you are and know you are. Ali was using affirmations publicly, to full effect, before they were as popular as they are today.

He Convinced Himself

This example is used here because it is one of the most public examples of affirmations in action. It also shows what can be achieved if they are used correctly. Not alone did Muhammad Ali convince the world that he was the greatest but more importantly, he convinced himself.

He went on to prove himself both inside and outside the boxing ring. He became not just the greatest boxer of all time, he was a poet of note, a philanthropist and a very powerful and influential human being. He also appears to have been an all-round decent human being – that is, so long as you didn't get into the boxing ring with him.

One Example

This is just one example of affirmations in action. It shows what can and will happen when you use affirmations correctly, in the pursuit of your goals and dreams. When using affirmations for a specific purpose, it is best not to announce it to the world this will only put unnecessary pressure on you.

When Muhammad Ali (Cassius Clay) was using his affirmations, he was in a very dangerous and competitive business – professional boxing. To get the maximum personal benefit from what he was doing, he convinced himself, his opponents, the media and everyone else that he was the greatest.

When you use affirmations, most of the time you will only have to convince yourself. Therefore, when you use affirmations, it is probably best not to make any public announcements. Unlike Muhammad Ali, you will not have to convince the world that you are the greatest, you will only have to convince yourself.

Create Your Own

The following list will help you create affirmations. Like the gratitude list mentioned earlier this is also a great exercise and it will lift your spirits. It will help improve your self-talk and is a very healthy practice to cultivate. The practice of creating your own affirmations will help you develop healthy thinking and lessen the chances of slipping back into the doldrums. Use the following list to help get you started. Once you get familiar with this kind of language it will get simpler. You will eventually be able to come up with powerful affirmations in seconds for any occasion. Start creating affirmations now, write:

I attract peace and tranquillity into my life.
I love having peace...
I am calm...
The conflict is over for me...
I am peaceful...
I am kind...
I am tolerant... I am compassionate...

I Am "not" I Will Be

When writing affirmations, remember that they are always written in the present tense. For example, *I am safe and secure under all conditions* not I will be safe and secure when conditions are better. The "I am" is very important. You will find more information on affirmations throughout this book and on the internet. Don't forget the best affirmations are the ones you create yourself as they will best suit your needs.

Check Out

For more on creating and using affirmations, check out, *You Can Heal Your Life* by Louise L. Hay, The Game of Life and How to Play It by Florence Scovel-Shinn, NLP The New Technology of Achievement by Steve Andreas and Charles Faulkner. These are just a few books connected to the subject of affirmations.

CHAPTER TWELVE

Progress and Expectations

When you start to practise the three core steps, you will begin to experience life differently. Happiness, contentment, well-being, wealth and poverty will start to take on a new meaning for you. In this chapter the discussion will centre around what you might expect as your journey towards greater well-being and peace of mind continues.

Even at this early stage of your transformation, you will actually begin to feel the first signs of spirituality beginning to emerge. For many, this condition will be exactly the sign you are looking for, to motivate you to keep going.

For others, progress can be more challenging and because of the lack of familiarity and connectivity with the spiritual side of your being, you may even think you are going backwards. It is the lack of familiarity that can cause you to cling on to old thoughts and feelings and that old way of living, even if it is making your life hell.

Tuning In to Your own Thoughts

As you begin to make progress one of the many things that will occur is that you will begin to become more in tune with your own thoughts. You will start to recognise your own thoughts and move away from doing other people's thinking.

You may be thinking to yourself, right now, that you are always in tune with your own thoughts. Ask yourself, have you ever found yourself saying or thinking something like, "they think that I'm going to do that" or, "I think that they think" or, "they think that I think"?

These are simple examples of doing other people's thinking. The point being, if you are doing other people's thinking you are not in tune with your own thoughts. As you continue your progress, watch out for this and practise the core steps to avoid doing other people's thinking. Practise:

> **Name it**: I am doing other people's thinking. I am now letting go of these thoughts.
> **Share it**: I am doing other people's thinking. I am now letting go of these thoughts.
> **Replace it**: I think my own thoughts only. I do my own thinking. Repeat!

Connecting with Your own Feelings

During the course of a lifetime many people get out of touch with their own feelings. This can result in losing the ability to feel anything at all and basically becoming numb to, not just the extremes of feelings but the general joys and sorrows of the human experience. As a result of practising the core steps and the other suggestions, you will start to become more aware of your own feelings.

If you are completely new to working on your feelings, it can be a testing experience and will require a bit of getting used to. Once you have practised the core steps on a feeling, you can gradually introduce yourself to the idea of sitting with a feeling for a while. This basically means sitting with the feeling for a few seconds, before you let it go. There is no point in trying to run from feelings because sooner or later they will catch up with you. All you have to do is name them, share them and replace them.

In most cases, sitting with a feeling for a while is not a problem however, if the feeling is very intense, you may need someone to help you with this. This can be a professional, an experienced listener or someone who is already experienced in the practice of these steps.

Expect Your Confidence to Grow

As you make progress, your lack of familiarity will be replaced by the knowledge that you are able to deal with any situation that arises in your life. You will start to experience a new kind of peace and contentment and begin to enjoy life in the present moment. The more you practise, the more your confidence will grow and the stronger you will feel. You will begin to feel more at peace with yourself and the world around you.

You will experience great changes for the better and will have a greater desire to continue your progress. Although you may not, as yet, have considered your progress beyond your material existence, which is the physical and psychological level of your being, you will start to become aware that there is more to you than a body with a mind. You have other faculties and in the later chapters this concept is explored on a deeper level.

You May Not Want To

You may experience the urge to resist the changes taking place in you. Strange as it may seem, there may be times when you may not want to let go of a troublesome feeling, attitude, thought or emotion or an old idea. Believe it or not, some people get attached and take comfort from what is actually harming them.

It is as if the pain has become the painkiller. This is similar to what occurs when an attachment becomes addictive. Even though the old thoughts, feelings and ideas are destroyers of all that is healthy, they can be difficult to let go. This can be because troublesome thoughts and feelings can become so much a part of you that they become a comfort.

To deal with these attachments and other addictive issues, apply the steps and try to identify exactly what you are feeling and thinking. You will find more helpful suggestions on addictions and troubled thinking in Chapter 15.

A Problem Shared

When you begin practising the steps and some of the other suggestions, you will begin to feel well. This will happen even if you are not yet fully practising the steps. This means that once you start practising step one you will feel some benefit. This is a good thing but it can have an unintended effect. For example you may be tempted not to do the most important thing which is to share as in step two. To avoid this, try to share as quickly as possible once you apply step one.

Sharing is essential for long term well-being. It is one of the best tools available to you and will ensure your continued success. The more you share, the more progress you will make and the less surprises you will have. As the three steps are the core of this approach, so too is sharing the core of the three steps. Sharing is the channel through which fellowship flows and grows.

As mentioned earlier "a problem shared is a problem halved"? Beyond that when you share the same problem again, it will be halved again. In other words the more you share the more progress you will make and the more relief you will experience.

Remember to share, share, share! You can't share enough. You can call or e-mail Samaritans, or any of the other groups mentioned in this book to share. You can do this anonymously at any time to share your troublesome thoughts and feelings if you do not have someone to share with yet.

Look for the Good

As you continue on your journey, you may come across people who act and speak in a negative or unhelpful way to you. If possible, it is best to avoid interaction with such people until you are feeling stronger. However, this may not always be possible so, you will also need another strategy. This will involve looking for the good in everything no matter how dreadful the situation may appear.

Let's say you are in company and the conversation turns negative, don't engage with it. Change the conversation the moment you get a chance. You could say something like, "You're looking well today" or, "That's a lovely colour". In other words say anything so long as it is decent. Use your surroundings to pick something pleasant to say for example "that's a nice plant". This will work for you and help you feel better about yourself.

At first, this strategy can feel a bit strange but with practice, looking for the good will be like taking a giant step forward in how you feel. If you apply this strategy at every opportunity, you will also be sharing a great gift with everyone you have contact with and you will feel better about yourself and life in general.

Looking Ahead

As your progress continues, you will start to recognise those feelings, attitudes, thoughts and emotions that can cause trouble ahead if not dealt with early. Being able to recognise potential difficulties early will allow you the time to deal with them before they become major obstacles in your life. This means that you will be able to prevent some of the most harmful thoughts and feelings taking hold and stopping your progress.

Being able to look ahead and keep clear of as many hazards as possible will shorten the road for you and stack the cards in your favour, in all areas of your life. Having the tools to navigate the best possible route to happiness and greater well-being will greatly reduce the stresses and strains of any hurdles you may encounter. Practising this process correctly will even eliminate certain problems altogether if you have the willingness and desire to be happy and free.

Relationships

The practice of this approach to contentment will take you to a new level of existence in all your relationships. At this stage, you are probably beginning to realise that this is not just a few exercises you can do today and forget tomorrow. It is in fact a way of life that offers a way of living that allows you to be yourself and make the needed changes in your life with the least amount of effort. These changes will be noticed by those around you and all your relationships will benefit. You will begin to attract new people into your life who are also on a similar path and new relationships will develop.

One of the very challenging areas of human life is that of attracting love and the right people. The question is often asked, how? How do you attract the right kind of people into your life? First, you need to ask yourself the following question. What kind of people do I want to attract? Do you want angry, lazy, miserable people or kind, compassionate, loving people?

If you want to attract people who are kind and loving, then you must develop these qualities in yourself. These are attracting qualities and will attract others into your life who are of the same persuasion. This is the way it works! If you want to attract a kind and loving person into your life, then you must become a kind and loving person.

Attracting Love

The same principles apply to all relationships. If you want your relationships to be loving, then you must become loving. If you want love in your life, you must practise love and the first person you must love is yourself. The fact is if you do not love yourself, you will not be able to love someone else and what's more you will not let someone else love you. Remember, love grows where love goes.

So, start by being kind and compassionate towards yourself. These qualities are expressions of a spiritual being and are the essence of unconditional love. When you practise these qualities towards yourself and then extend them to those around you, the kind of person you are will become obvious to all who come into contact with you and they will want to be in your company. In this way, you will attract those who are first of all able to love themselves and in turn will then be able to love you.

Be patient with yourself in this area and keep in mind, you can't fake love. Love attracts and love grows in loving relationships otherwise, it is not love.

Wisdom

As you begin to make progress on your journey being aware of the relationship that exists between what you know and what you think you know is important. You will also need to be aware of the different kinds of people in the world, so that you can separate what is true for you from what is false.

The ability to separate what is true from what is false is a hallmark of the wise. The wisdom of the past will help you to get a perspective on yourself and other people and how you might fit into the bigger picture. The Persian poet, Ibn Yamin, back in the 13th century, suggested there were four categories of people:

Those who know and know they know (wisdom)
Those who know but don't know they know (asleep)
Those who don't know but know they don't know (they will get there slowly)
Those who don't know but don't know they don't know (lost).

Using This Wisdom

In 2002, Donald Rumsfeld, the then US Secretary of Defence, used some of the wisdom of Ibn Yamin during a press conference relating to the war in Iraq when he said in part:

"There are known known's: things we know we know. There are known unknowns, that is to say, there are things we know we don't know but, there are also unknown unknowns: things we don't know we don't know."

He goes on to say that it is the unknown unknowns that tend to be the most difficult to deal with. This statement initially sent journalists into a bit of a spin trying to figure out what on earth he was on about.

The good news is that you don't have to figure out what he was on about. What is important to realise now is that, like most human beings, there is so much you know but don't yet know you know. This is basically because most are asleep or indifferent to this fact and need to wake up before it is too late. The practice of this process will wake you up to this fact and one day, the penny will drop and you will know you know. This is what wisdom is; knowing you know!

Knowing

You cannot get the full benefit from thinking you know or half-knowing something. This is because, while you are in this halfway condition, you will always be doubting yourself and everyone else.

The practice of the core steps, the exercises and the other suggestions will help you move closer to a level of knowing, which is more like wisdom. If you stick with it, you will eventually be able to differentiate what attracts and is good for you, from what repels and is damaging for you, no matter where it comes from. When you arrive at this level of knowing, you will start to experience the effect of wisdom. You will become part of the Ibn Yamin classification of people who know and know they know.

At this stage, you will be enjoying the changes taking place in your life and you will be starting to realise that you are much more than a body with a mind; you are a spiritual human being.

Making Progress

If you watch or listen long enough to even the most accomplished people, no matter how great they are, you will eventually see and hear their limitations. The point being that nobody is perfect. You will always end up being disappointed if you place your belief in other people. Ultimately, you have to seek so that you can find your own answers and experience well-being through your own efforts. In this way, you will come to know a life of confidence, happiness and peace of mind. Making progress is what this approach is all about, not about being perfect.

CHAPTER THIRTEEN

Do's and Don'ts

When doing any kind of self-development, it is not unusual to arrive at a point where you may try to resist the changes that you are making. For example, you may find yourself wanting to hold on to old feelings, attitudes, thoughts and emotions. Holding on to old ideas is a form of resistance and will slow down your progress. This is among the do's and don'ts you will come across on your journey.

The do's are among the actions you should embrace, as they will have the effect of speeding up your progress. The don'ts, on the other hand, should be avoided as they will slow down your progress if you practise them. It is not possible to account for all the things you should do and those that need to be avoided. Nevertheless, a number of do's and don'ts will be discussed in this chapter.

Like everything else in these pages, this chapter too is essential reading. If you want to have happiness and peace of mind you need to know the do's and the don'ts. Some of these are very subtle and arrive unannounced. This is not a problem in the case of the do's. On the other hand, when it comes to the don'ts you need to become aware of their presence as quickly as possible. An example of a don't would be fault finding. This is a human trait you need to be aware of so that you can deal with it.

Finding What's Wrong

Many people engage in fault finding unintentionally and this is one of the don'ts that can sneak up on you and quickly bring your progress to a halt. The daily practice and affirmation of what you see as wrong in your life and the world around you will leave you feeling sad and miserable.

Fault finding is similar to gossip but it differs in that it may not always involve the affairs of other people. It can but not always. It is more about looking for what is wrong in all areas of life, to such an extent that eventually, no good can be seen in anything. It may involve something as simple as being irritated by the weather, a dripping tap, the colour of someone's clothes, a blocked drain, it can be anything.

The point is, if you practise an attitude of fault finding and continuously affirm it by talking about what is wrong with everything, that is the way it will be for you. This kind of negativity can be infectious and needs to be avoided as a matter of urgency. Do use the core steps to change this attitude.

Looking for the Good

After the naming and sharing of the fault-finding attitude in steps one and two. It can now be replaced in step three with the following affirmation or a similar one to replace the fault-finding attitude:

Replace it: I see the good in everything and everyone. Repeat!

If you continuously look for the good then that is what you will eventually see. It is always good practice to look for and share about what is good in your life and the world around you. Some days, it may be difficult to see the good in anything but if you persevere you will find it. Remember the best way to begin seeing the good in everything is to use the steps because this will allow you to identify and let go of the old attitude before replacing it with the new.

Your Words Become Your Habits

If negative and harmful words and statements are repeated continuously, they will affect how you feel and think. Use them often enough and they will eventually become the norm for you. Negative and harmful language should, therefore, be removed from your vocabulary in as much as it is possible. On the other hand, the use of healthy and positive language and affirmations will also become habitual if used often enough. The practice of affirmations should be continued until they are part of your being.

Remove any negative language and harmful words towards yourself using steps one and two then replace them with a positive affirmation in step three:

> **Replace it**: I always use positive and helpful language towards myself and others. Repeat!

Cultivating Willingness to Change

You will also need to be willing and open to change. If you are having difficulty finding the willingness you can apply the steps and use affirmations to help you get motivated. Use the following affirmation after you have applied steps one and two:

> **Replace it**: I am willing to change.

By the way, remember the magic twenty-one number! If you are having real difficulty in developing willingness, try saying the affirmation twenty-one times. Continue this practice for twenty-one days. To turn the affirmation into a way of life, continue the practice for ninety days. You can also try this with other affirmations. This will help you to foster and develop a greater willingness to change. For example:

I am open to change.
I am willing to change. I am willing to try.

Experiment with these affirmations, change the words, change them around, make them yours. Repeat them often. If you use these affirmations as an independent exercise repeat often and don't forget to pause between repetitions. For more on using affirmations check out *You Can Heal Your Life* by Louise L. Hay.

I Am

Saying the "I am" is a very important part of doing the steps and using affirmations. For example, in the practice of step one, a lot of the time you will start your affirmations by saying, "I am…". Saying "I am…" has far deeper meanings than can be seen at first glance. With practice, the wisdom of this will become known.

Check out Wayne Dyer's book, *Wishes Fulfilled* for more on the "I am" topic. You can also check out religious Scriptures for more on this subject and don't forget Descartes, "I think therefore I am."

Right now however, try saying the following and creating your own "I am" affirmations:

I am grateful…
I am happy…
I am…

Surrender

Many years ago, Joe was a very angry, anxious and fearful man. He was at war with the world and everyone in it but, he didn't know it. Then, one day, a friend of his, Jane, who was a life coach, whispered in Joe's ear, "Joe the war is over …"

To add insult to injury she went on to say, "… and guess what, Joe? You lost."

For the first time in his life, Joe heard what was said. He realised that all his life he had been at war with himself and the whole world but, he didn't know.

His friend, Jane, suggested he surrender. At first, Joe was reluctant to even consider such an option until one day, he could not take anymore. He called his friend, Jane and said the magic words, "I am beaten; I don't want to fight anymore."

This was the first time that Joe acknowledged to himself and admitted to someone else that he was beaten. That day, he raised the white flag of surrender and immediately felt relief. Soon, he started to see that he had been at war with himself all his life. He started using the following affirmation:

I surrender; the war is over for me.

The Power of Surrender

Although it took a while for Joe to realise the depth of what he was doing he quickly realised that this defeat was a victory in disguise. He didn't know it at the time but he had just discovered the power of surrender. He raised the white flag and never went to war with his thoughts and feelings again.

He discovered too that surrender was the fast track to lasting happiness and peace of mind. It is one of the greatest assets to have at your disposal and once you apply it, it has immediate effect.

The concept of surrender is one of the great paradoxes in the world of personal development. Paradox in this sense means doing the opposite of what you think you should do to get the result you want. This means that if you are struggling with thoughts and feelings, the best way to beat them is to surrender. Do not fight or struggle with them instead, practise surrendering:

> Say, *I surrender. I no longer struggle with my thoughts and feelings.* Repeat often!

Smile

Another very important behaviour you should foster in your life is smiling. Charlie Chaplin got it right when he penned the lyrics of the great classic song, *Smile*. In it, he writes, "Smile though your heart is aching. Smile even though it's breaking…".

At the time of writing the song he may not have had the benefit of research to show just how right he was. Being a comedian he would have been well aware of the benefits of smiling and laughter. Research has since shown that smiling is very good for you and a very healthy practice. Even if your smile is fake it works. So do practise smiling, it will help you to feel better.

Just like all the other suggestions in this book, this one is also very simple. If you practise smiling often enough it will have a profound effect on how you feel and on those around you. If you like watching movies, try an old Charlie Chaplin movie, it will surely bring a smile to your face. You will find many of his movies and other comedies available online, and also on TV. Use whatever it takes to bring a smile to your face.

Happy and Peaceful

The following paragraphs are an essential reminder of the importance of living within certain standards and values. This topic has already been discussed in Chapter 7 but is revisited now because of its importance and the consequences of living outside of your personal values and societal standards.

Lasting happiness and peace of mind comes from living life within the boundaries of the personal values and standards you expect from yourself. There are also other values and laws within which you will have to live. These are set by the cultural, religious or ethnic community in which you live. If you break these community laws and values there will be societal penalties, for example, you may end up in prison.

There is another set of values and standards you will need to live by if you want permanent peace and happiness in your life. These are the values and standards you set for yourself. They may or may not be in agreement with the standards set by the society in which you live. Nevertheless, you must be willing to live by them if you want to have real happiness and peace of mind.

The penalty for breaching your own values and standards can be far greater than for a breach of any laws of a society. Therefore, to feel happy and peaceful in your life, you must be at least willing to avoid activities and behaviours that are outside your own personal values and standards.

The bottom line is, if you are acting outside of your own values, you will be miserable. Do try to live your life within your own values and standards. Of course, this also means that you should operate within the standard and values of the society in which you live.

Obstacles to Progress

There are a number of obstacles that you will have to deal with as you travel the road to peace of mind and greater well-being. Some of these will just slow your progress down; others will stop your progress altogether if they are not dealt with.

The continuous practice of any behaviour will eventually have an effect. That effect will be good or bad depending on what the behaviour is. Your actions have consequences and will affect you and all the people in your life directly and indirectly.

As you practise the three steps and the rest of this approach to well-being, you will also be either removing or changing behaviours that are likely to be obstacles to your progress. Therefore, do try to act and behave in a way that will not hinder your progress. If you are willing and keep practising, you will always be making progress, even when you think you are going backwards.

As You Think

There is a saying from Scripture that goes something like, "As you think so shall you be". This has been used to great effect by Dr Wayne Dyer in his work of passing on the message of hope to the world. The saying itself has its origin in the Bible and Buddhist scripture.

Mahatma Gandhi has also highlighted the importance of using your thoughts wisely. He tells us that "your thoughts become your words; your words become your actions." The point is that your thoughts and your actions are very closely linked, so much so, that it is said that you become what you think about. So, do not spend your time in morbid thinking or on what is wrong in the world. Focus on what is good.

If you spend your time thinking of ways to avoid your family, thinking about socialising with other people or thinking about the difficulties in life, then that is what you will show up in your life. On the other hand, if you focus on thinking about having fun with family and the wholesome things in life, that is what you will attract into your life. This is just making the point that what you think about, you will eventually act on. As the wisdom of the past tells us, "As you think, so shall you be."

The Highway and Roundabout

How you feel affects your actions and behaviour. In turn your actions and behaviour affect how you feel. This can be seen as a circular flow of feelings, attitude, thoughts, emotions and actions. Sooner or later, how you feel becomes an attitude, a thought and eventually, an emotional response acted out in your behaviour. It also works the other way round. Your actions and behaviour affect how you feel, your attitude, your thinking and your emotional responses.

In this sense life can be seen as an endless open highway of changing actions, behaviours, thoughts and feelings. On this highway there is an infinite number of roundabouts full of changing feelings attitudes thoughts and emotions. Your actions and behaviour sooner or later lead you to a roundabout full of feelings, attitude thoughts and emotions (FATE).

Your actions and behaviour on this endless highway will decide what kind of FATE awaits you on the roundabouts. If your actions and behaviours are within your own value system your experience on the roundabouts will be happy and peaceful. You will have no problem continuing your journey. If not, you will have to deal with many troublesome thoughts and feelings and dread the journey ahead.

If you arrive at a roundabout on this metaphorical highway of life and your thinking is all over the place you will need to practise the three steps to get you back on the road. In this way you can let go of the troublesome thoughts and feelings that are keeping you stuck on a roundabout. Managing your thoughts and feelings in this way will get you back on the road quickly.

Just like your actions and behaviour out on the highway will decide what awaits you on a roundabout so too how you manage your FATE on the roundabouts will affect your actions and behaviour on the highway. It's the spherical flow of feelings, attitudes, thoughts, emotions and behaviours. How you think, feel and act are so closely linked as to be one and the same and will in the end decide your FATE. Do keep this in mind as your journey continues.

Gossip

Gossip is soul destroying it's one of the big no "nose" and should be avoided at all costs. Outside of the fact that you are destroying someone else's character, you are also letting your listeners know what kind of person you are. If you choose to say something nasty about another human being, one of the things you are actually doing is telling the listener what kind of person you are and that you are not trustworthy. Of course, listening to gossip is not much better than gossip itself. Gossip is the destroyer of all that is good and its negative effects can last for generations.

Resentment

Resentment is also something that needs to be stamped out. It has been described by some as being like "drinking a bottle of poison and hoping someone else dies." By being resentful towards someone, you are hurting yourself. Practise the three steps on any resentment that shows up in your life.

There is a great story told in relation to resentment that says something like, "nobody ever dies from a snake bite. It's the venom left behind after you've been bitten that kills."

The venom is the resentment left behind after you have been hurt by someone. You must get that venom out of your system. You will be able to identify hidden resentments by carrying out an emotional stocktaking inventory. Then let them go using the three steps.

If You're Not There, It Can't Happen

When you begin your journey towards peace of mind and happiness, there are certain places and things that are best avoided. You may have heard it said, "If you're not there, it can't happen." What this boils down to is that there will be certain places, situations, people, activities and behaviours that you would do best to avoid when making any changes in your life.

This means you should avoid scenarios or contacts that stir up troublesome thoughts and feelings. This is not a permanent solution but it should last long enough for you to have found the strength to deal with whatever may arise. Examples of these situations may include avoiding aggressive people, events where alcohol or other drugs are being consumed, casinos and betting shops if you are trying to avoid gambling.

Your Fate

Your fate is a fundamental part of this discussion therefore you need to know a few things about it so that you can benefit from it and not be afraid of it. In this book fate is simply another word for destiny. Your fate is directly influenced by how you manage your feelings, attitudes, thoughts and emotions (FATE). This means that you can change your FATE any time that you want to.

However, there are two kinds of fate. In one of these you have no control for example, you are compelled to eat and sleep. You have no control over this part of your fate. The other kind of fate relates to your feelings, attitude, thoughts and emotions in this you have control. In fact you have complete control!

This part of your fate is all about your feelings, attitudes, thoughts and emotions but it doesn't end there it is also about how you act and behave. Therefore peace of mind, happiness and overall well-being is dependent on how well you manage both your FATE and your actions and behaviour.

This means that when you are managing your feelings, attitudes, thoughts, emotions, actions and behaviours you are also managing your happiness and contentment. And because your FATE, your actions and behaviours are so closely connected, when you are deciding on how you are going to act and behave you are actually creating your own destiny in relation to whether you will be happy and contented or just plain miserable. Check out *Closer Than Your Life Vein* by Henry A. Weil for further discussion.

Getting the Basics Right

Getting the basics right in any discipline is essential to your ongoing progress. Having knowledge of what you are doing, how you are going to do it and why you are doing it, will help to ensure that you get the full benefit of what you are doing.

As with learning anything new, when you start to practise this approach to well-being, it will feel strange and awkward. However, once you have the basics right and practise regularly, you will quickly master it. The steps are designed to be easy to learn and simple to use therefore, the process will quickly become familiar to you.

At first, it may appear complex but this is just because there are many exercises and suggestions coming at you all at once. With practice, you will quickly come to know and enjoy this process. This is because you will begin to feel the overall positive effects on your well-being. You will begin to develop new relationships. You will start to see the healthy differences in the lives of those closest to you; your family, friends and loved ones. These benefits all begin with just getting the basics right.

You Are Not Alone

One last, very important point to keep in mind as you continue on your journey towards peace and happiness keep in mind you are not alone in managing your thoughts and feelings. You can say goodbye to loneliness and isolation once you are willing to practise the three steps and adding as many of the other exercises on to your personal development toolkit.

You are welcome to contact me at any time. You can do this through the website. There is also the Samaritans, along with other groups and professionals available to you around the world. There is also much more to discover as your journey continues.

Hopefully by now you are starting to have the conversation with at least one other person you may be able to share with. In the meantime don't forget the helplines if you need someone right now.

CHAPTER FOURTEEN

Time Out and Mindfulness

In this chapter, you will first be introduced to the concept and practice of Time Out. This is a very simple exercise to practise and can be used anywhere, anytime. It is primarily used to switch off your thoughts and feelings for a couple of seconds. This can be very useful when you need to take a short break from the stresses and demands of a day.

An approach to Mindfulness and Awareness will also be introduced and you will discover two widely used mindfulness meditations: Sati and Metta. These meditations are part of this book because they are particularly useful in the management of thoughts and feelings.

It is not really possible to convey the intricacies of mindfulness meditation in this brief chapter but, you will get enough insight to help you get underway in the practice of Mindfulness. If you want to explore these meditations on a deeper level, check out the possibility of doing a training course in mindfulness meditation.

Time Out, Mindfulness and Awareness Meditations are wonderful personal development tools in their own right but they will not be enough on their own to deal with troublesome feelings, attitudes, thoughts and emotions. Therefore, along with the techniques offered in this chapter you will still need to keep practising the three steps and as many of the other suggestions as possible. This is essential if you want to have lasting peace of mind and real happiness in your life.

Time Out is explained first, followed by a more in-depth discussion about Mindfulness, Awareness and Meditation techniques. Then, at the end of the chapter, you will be provided with an outline of the mindfulness meditation procedures. You will be able to use this outline as a guide during your meditation sessions, until you have memorised the process.

Time Out

Imagine what it would be like to be able to switch off your thoughts and feelings instantly. If you practise Time Out correctly, that is exactly what you will be able to do. First, you must learn how to practise then, all you have to do is, do it. It functions mainly as a switch but when you are more familiar with it you can turn it into a longer meditation if you wish.

For now though, think of Time Out as a control switch designed to enable you to turn off your thoughts and feelings anytime you want. This can be at work, at home, at play, before an interview, after an interview, before an exam, during any kind of event or whatever situation you find yourself in.

Using Time Out, you will be able to switch off your thoughts and feelings, regain composure and get back on track quickly. Practise as often as you can until you master it. It takes no more than fifteen seconds to do, therefore it will fit into even the busiest of lifestyles. The idea is to practise it until it becomes a spontaneous response to the stressful events of a day.

How to Practise Time Out

You can do this exercise sitting down or standing up, at home, at work, on a bus or on a train or anywhere you want. If you do it standing up, hold on to something or keep your eyes open to avoid losing your balance.

In your first Time Out practice, you will be sitting and listening to a sound you choose. It might be the sound of traffic, the engine of a bus, a train engine, somebody talking, the wind, the rain, the thunder it can be any sound, it can even be the sound of silence. Let's say you pick the sound of traffic.

Example 1
In a sitting position close your eyes take a deep breath and as you inhale in your mind say,

I am aware of the sound of traffic.

Exhale slowly then gradually open your eyes. Continue with whatever you are doing. Time: 15 seconds.

It takes no more than fifteen seconds. You can do this exercise as often as you like throughout your day and you will feel the benefits. Try it now!

Using the Sound of Silence
You can also listen for the sound of silence. This one may take a little bit of getting used to.

Example 2
In a sitting position close your eyes take a deep breath and as you inhale say to yourself:

I am aware of the sound of silence.

Exhale slowly then gradually open your eyes. Continue what you were doing.

Remember you can do it as often as you like.

Time Frame
It is important to stick to this time frame and take no more than fifteen seconds to practise a single Time Out. Remember the purpose of Time Out is to enable you to

switch off your thoughts and feelings for a few seconds not go into a deep meditation.

Sound and Silence

You can use silence even if there is lots of noise going on around you. Though it may take a bit of getting used to. Keep in mind that every sound comes out of silence if there were no silence there would be no sound. Sometimes it may be hard to hear the silence amidst the noise of modern life, but it's there and you will be able to hear it with practice and patience.

Standing

If you do a Time Out standing up you must hold on to something to make sure you do not fall over. The other option is to keep your eyes open again this is to prevent you from losing your balance and falling over. So remember, you can practise this exercise sitting down or standing up, anytime, anywhere and as many times as you like, but if you do it standing up you must hold on to something or keep your eyes open.

Switch Off

The purpose of this exercise is to learn how to "switch off" your thoughts and feelings. Regular practice will enable you to be more affective at doing this switching. It will also energise you and allow you to regain your composure during those stressful days.

To achieve this level of control you will need to practise until it becomes a spontaneous action. Being able to switch of your thoughts and feelings in this way will increase your energy levels and improve your overall feeling of well-being. It will allow you to be more focused, aware and responsive in whatever situation you find yourself in.

It will help to reduce feelings of stress, anxiety and helplessness before or during a performance or task you may be working on. The more you practise the more you will be able to use this switch effectively.

One other important thing about Time Out is that you can practise it on your own or in a crowded room and nobody need know you switched off for a few seconds.

Mindfulness

Mindfulness is another wonderful tool to have available for the purpose of keeping thoughts and feelings and the general stresses and strains of life under control. Regular practice of mindfulness, along with the three core steps and the other suggestions, will help you to cultivate and sustain peace of mind, excellent mental health and greater overall feelings of well-being.

It is not possible to have a meaningful discussion about mindfulness without also talking about Awareness, Meditation and Buddhism.

Mindfulness, Awareness and Meditation

Mindfulness, Awareness and Meditation go hand in hand. There are many forms of mindfulness meditation. The practice itself is very popular and is associated with Buddhism.

There are two forms of Mindfulness Meditation popular in the west: Sati Meditation and Metta Meditation. An approach to these two forms of Mindfulness Meditation will be introduced later. These have been adapted from traditional Buddhist practices.

Although mindfulness, awareness and meditation are closely linked to practices in Buddhism and indeed, Hinduism, it is important to understand that the practice of meditation, in one form or another, has been in existence as long as mankind has existed.

In some ethnic groups, meditation has a more central role than in others. However, if you look closely enough meditation in one form or another shows up wherever there are human beings. In some cultures, it may not be recognised formally as meditation but nevertheless contemplation, meditation and reflection show up in the traditions of every culture and religion.

Whether it's the Dance of the Native American, the Gregorian Chant of Christian Monks, the Dance of the Sufi Whirling Dervishes or the Meditations of a Buddhist Monk makes no difference. Having the capacity to meditate, reflect and contemplate is part of what makes you a human being.

Defining Mindfulness

A very simple working definition of mindfulness is given by Padraig O'Morain, author of *Mindfulness on the Go*, who says that mindfulness is "being aware of what you are doing while you are doing it." This definition gives a starting point on the way to a more sophisticated understanding of what mindfulness is.

The next step towards a higher level of understanding, is to remember that mindfulness is not just about your "doings". It is probably more about your "being". Mindfulness is being present and paying attention, as an unbiased observer, of your own feelings, attitudes, thoughts, emotions, actions and physical sensations as they occur, in the present moment.

Awareness?

Mindfulness is so closely associated with awareness that one would be forgiven for thinking that they are the same thing. With this in mind they will now be separated and explored further.

Where Did I Leave my Glasses?

On the one hand, Awareness in the context of Mindfulness is not easy to define but on the other, the lack of awareness is easy to spot. Think about how often you have put something somewhere and shortly afterwards, it was nowhere to be found, for example, your glasses or your keys. Practising Awareness will mean less time looking for your glasses, your keys or, at times, even your car.

Awareness Meditation

You will shortly be introduced to a very simple awareness meditation. If you are completely new to any of the following meditations there are some things you need to know that will make your experience more fulfilling. First these meditations are very different from listening to meditative music or some form of guided meditation. These all have their uses and their place but they are very different.

In Mindfulness and Awareness meditations the only aid you will need is your own awareness. This means you will be conscious of where you are and what's going on at all times. When you are going into deeper levels of meditation you will be the observer of your mind, your body and your own experience.

One of the issues you will have to deal with during your meditation is the urge to move. Obviously, you will have to do so if you are extremely uncomfortable therefore, if you have to move you will need to do it slowly. Eventually you will be able to remain still for the duration of your meditation. It may take time to develop enough trust in the process to let go completely. In the meantime keep in mind that any attempt to meditate will be of benefit to you.

A Simple Awareness Meditation

To practise this Awareness meditation you will need to find a place where you will not be disturbed. Sit on a chair, lie on a couch or bed, whatever is available and comfortable. Remove your shoes and loosen any tight clothing to make yourself as comfortable as possible.

When you are ready, you will close your eyes and just become aware of the sounds that you hear. As in the practice of Time Out, this sound can be any kind of noise. As mentioned already it can even be the sound of silence. When listening for the sound of noise you will not have a problem, you will hear plenty noise. However, as you learned from the practice of time out, you may find listening for the sound of silence a bit of a challenge.

To help you in this challenge you are reminded again to keep in mind that without silence there would be no sound. All sounds come from the silence therefore silence is everywhere. You will eventually get the hang of it. For now, just try to follow the guidelines.

This can be a bit like learning to ride a bicycle you may fall a few times but once you get up and try again, you'll eventually be able to do it. All it takes is a bit of perseverance and a bit of guidance and you are ready.

To Practise this Awareness Meditation

You will need to be in a place where you will not be disturbed and sitting on a chair. When you are ready make yourself comfortable, close your eyes take one or two deep breaths and say each of the affirmations below in your mind. You will stay with each affirmation for fifteen or twenty seconds before moving on to the next one:

> *I am aware of the sounds I hear outside.*
> *I am aware of the silence I hear outside.*
> *I am aware of the sounds I hear inside.*
> *I am aware of the silence I hear inside.*
> *I am aware of the chair supporting me.*
> *I am aware of my feet on the ground.*

Time: 2 minutes

Take no more than two minutes to practise this meditation. You can practise it lying on a bed or on a couch as well as on a chair. If you are doing this meditation lying on a bed change the wording of the last two affirmations as necessary:

> *I am aware of the bed (couch) supporting me.*
> *I am aware of my body resting on the bed (couch).*

When you are finished, open your eyes slowly and stretch gently. Caution! Try not to move too suddenly after any meditation. This is because your muscles have been switched off and need to be turned back on again slowly to avoid injury. Reminder! This applies to all meditations, whether short or long.

Note: This meditation is also used as the preamble for the longer meditations in this chapter. It is set out as a preamble at the end of this chapter.

Long or Short

You can practise this exercise as a short meditation for a couple of minutes and then open your eyes. It can also be turned into a longer meditation by just repeating each affirmation three or more times pausing between each repetition. As mentioned earlier, do not move too suddenly after any meditation, no matter how long or short. Sudden movement after being motionless, for any length of time, can easily cause an injury.

This advice may appear over cautious when you first start to meditate but it is best to err on the side of caution. Start as you mean to go on. It is much easier to introduce good practice habits when you are starting something new than it is to try and correct bad habits after they have been established.

Mindfulness: Sati and Metta

You will now be introduced to an approach to two forms of Mindfulness Meditation, called Sati and Metta. They are widely used and usually practised together. The Sati form is used to calm the mind in preparation for the Metta meditation, which works on feelings and emotions. Although they are usually practised together, you can also do them as individual meditations.

In a general practice session lasting one hour, thirty minutes of Sati would be followed by thirty minutes of Metta. In the approach presented here, your practice sessions will last ten minutes each. In actual practice, they can last as long as you want them to. However if you are completely new to this form of meditation it is best to start with shorter versions. In this introduction, you will be practising ten minutes of Sati and ten minutes of Metta.

Sati Meditation

As just mentioned, the purpose of Sati meditation is to clear and calm your mind. This is achieved using a simple counting technique. When you begin to practise the technique, your mind will try to resist. The reason for this resistance is that the counting exercise itself is really mundane and boring and your mind will not want to do it. With practice, you will be able to bring your mind under your control within a few minutes and, eventually, within seconds.

As with anything you are trying to master, it is essential to practise correctly, otherwise you will just be practising your mistakes. Correct practice will bring rich rewards.

To Practise Sati

To practise your Sati meditation there are a few things you need. First, you will need a place where you will have privacy where you can sit or lie without being disturbed. Next, you will need a chair, couch or bed to sit or lie on. You will also need a timer of some sort.

Privacy

Although for formal meditation a place of privacy is best but this does not mean you have to be alone to meditate. You can meditate while others are around but if you are teaching yourself using this, or any other book it may be difficult to do if you are not alone. Privacy is the best option if you are just starting to learn on your own but this may not be available to everyone. To overcome this maybe you could encourage those around you to learn to meditate with you. This would be a great way to learn.

Chair, Couch, Bed

You can use a chair, couch or bed for all the meditations in this book. They can be practised sitting up or lying down. In this guide the emphasis is placed on comfort rather than on tradition. Be that as it is, good posture and tradition will be briefly explored in the next couple of paragraphs to help shed some light on these important aspects of mindfulness meditation.

Good Posture

In this approach to meditation, there is no real emphasis put on posture. However, this is not to take away from the importance of, and the need for good posture in the practice of your meditations. The reality is that there are many different postures associated with the purest form of mindfulness meditation. You are free to experiment with these later if you wish. For now, the purpose is to introduce you to the basics of this type of meditation, so that you can begin your practice straight away.

The point here is that, whatever posture you adopt and whatever form of meditation you decide to practise, you must ensure that you are comfortable. The reason for this is that during your meditation, you may be sitting still for a considerable length of time. Therefore, it is essential that you are comfortable, so that your body can relax and you do not have to make any unnecessary movements during the session.

Comfort and Tradition

If you are doing your meditation in a sitting position, you will still need to sit comfortably and never in a strained position. Always aim for comfort! In doing so you need not ignore tradition completely. For example, when seated place your left hand on your lap, palm facing up next, place the back of your right hand in the palm of your left hand. This is one of the traditional ways to hold your hands in the practice of true mindfulness meditation.

If you are lying down, make sure you lie comfortably in this case place your hands in a position where they are not obstructed or strained. You will then be ready to close your eyes and begin the Sati Preamble, which will involve saying affirmations slowly and exactly as they are written.

Timing Your Meditation

Counting is an essential part of the Sati practice and as this will be in five-minute blocks of time you will need to keep track of time during your meditations. For the purpose of timing, you will need a timer, an old-fashioned clock, watch or some kind of simple timing device is best suited.

Try to avoid using a mobile phone as a timer for this meditation. Actually it is best to switch your mobile phone off before you start and leave it in another room. This will eliminate at least one source of stress and interruption.

Before you begin your meditation session, the timer needs to be placed in a position where it can be seen, without moving anything other than your eyes. This is because you will have to open your eyes a number of times during each session and you will not want to move any other part of your body. Staying mindful of the time, in this way, will also help you keep your awareness throughout the meditation session.

The main reason for timing is that you will have to change the counting pattern every five minutes during the Sati meditation in addition the Metta meditations are also in five-minute blocks and need to be timed. If you were doing this type of meditation with a number of people, the group leader would use a small gong to remind you when the five-minute blocks of time were up.

About the Sati Preamble

The Sati Preamble is identical to the short Awareness meditation introduced earlier in this chapter. The purpose of the Sati Preamble is to get you into the right frame of mind for the main meditation. By the way, this preamble can be used as the precursor for any other longer meditations that you may decide to do. As you know, it consists of a number of very simple affirmations that need to be said exactly as they are written.

It is also important that you stick to the time schedule. This is because the preamble is only to set you up for the main meditation. Therefore, you will not want to spend too much time on it. Take no more than a few minutes to do the preamble. Always use the timer. Reminder! The timer should be a simple clock or watch, placed where you can see it easily when you open your eyes to check the time during your meditation session.

Stick to the script for now and do not change the wording or any part of the preamble or the main meditation, until you are absolutely certain you know what you are doing.

Introducing Sati the Process

The Sati meditation begins immediately after the preamble. During your meditation, you will be counting, in your mind, as you breathe therefore, you will need to become aware of your breathing.

To do this, watch your breathing for about ten seconds. Do not try to control it, just observe it. Then, as you inhale, in your mind say "one". Then as you inhale again, in your mind say "two". As you inhale again in your mind say "three" and so on, until you reach ten. Then go back to one and start counting again. Continue like this for five minutes.

After five minute you will begin counting as you exhale. To begin, in your mind, say "one" as you "exhale". Next, in your mind, say "two" as you "exhale" again. Next, in your mind say "three" as you "exhale" and so on, until you reach ten, then go back to one and start again. Continue counting like this for five minutes.

These two counting patterns of five minutes each gives you a total of ten minutes meditation. When you include the amount of time that it takes to do the preamble and a couple of minutes at the end of the meditation to warm down, it amounts to a fifteen-minute Sati meditation session.

Five-Minute Blocks of Time

It is common practice for a Sati meditation session to be twenty-five minutes long. This would amount to five blocks of five minutes each. Along with the preamble and warm down at the end of the session the meditation would last thirty minutes. In this example you are asked to do two five-minute blocks of time along with the preamble. When you are comfortable with the ten-minute session it can be extended easily by adding other five-minute blocks of time.

To Add Blocks of Time

To add additional blocks of time you can use the following examples. For the first additional five-minute block of time start counting as you inhale. In your mind say "one" as you "inhale" then say "two" as you "exhale". Next say "three" as you "inhale" then say "four" as you "exhale". Continue like this until you get to ten then go back to one and start again. Do this for five minutes.

For the next five-minute block in your mind say, "one" as you "exhale" then "two" as you "inhale" next say "three" as you "exhale" and so on until you reach ten, then go back to "one" and start again.

For the last five-minute block you can just observe your breathing. As you watch your breathing, in your mind say "in" as you "inhale" next, say "out" as you "exhale".

In total this amounts to a twenty-five-minute Sati meditation session, presented in five, five-minute blocks of time. Remember for these counting patterns all the counting takes place in your mind. Patience is required when memorising these exercises!

It is much simpler to practise this meditation than it is to explain it. You will find an outline of the Sati process set out at the end of this chapter to help you with this practice routine.

Dealing with Thoughts During Sati

The question is often asked, how do you deal with thoughts or feelings during your Sati meditation? The answer is very simple. Your mind will go wondering off to do its own thing. When this happens simply bring it back to "one" and begin counting again. In fact during some of your Sati meditations you may not even get past "two" before your mind starts drifting.

This is why it is important to keep in mind that the purpose of counting is to calm your mind not to count to ten. This is a common mistake made by many who are new to Sati meditation. So again the purpose of the counting is not to count to ten but to focus on the counting itself. You may never reach ten but, that does not matter.

What you need to know now is that when you start counting, thoughts will start to come into your mind almost immediately. When you become aware that you are thinking of something else, other than counting, simply stop, go back to "one" and start counting again. In this way, you will be setting and resetting your mind.

Whether you are a complete beginner or a very experienced meditator, as mentioned before you may not even get to two or three before you have to go back to one. This is perfectly okay. One more thing if, at any time, you find your counting has gone beyond "ten", immediately stop counting, go back to one and start again.

Time to Meditate

The Sati meditation is set out here along with the preamble, for you to browse and practise. It will take no more than fifteen minutes to do. It has two blocks of five minutes, along with the preamble and a few minutes warm down at the end. Make yourself comfortable and say the preamble:

Sati Preamble

I am aware of the sounds I hear outside.
I am aware of the sounds I hear inside.
I am aware of the silence I hear outside.
I am aware of the silence I hear inside.
I am aware of the chair supporting me.
I am aware of my feet on the ground.

Note! If you are doing this meditation lying on a bed or a couch, change the wording of the last two affirmations as follows:

I am aware of the bed (couch) supporting me.
I am aware of my hands and feet resting on the bed (couch).

Now is the time to make sure you are comfortable before you continue on to the main meditation.

Sati: The Two Blocks of Time

Block 1: Say "one" in your mind as you "inhale", then "two" in your mind as you "inhale", next "three" in your mind as you "inhale" and so on to "ten" then back to "one" and start again. Continue like this for five minutes.

Block 2: Say "one" in your mind as you "exhale" then "two" in your mind as you "exhale" next "three" in your mind as you "exhale" and so on to "ten" then go back to "one" and start again. Continue like this for five minutes.

Introducing Metta

It has been mentioned already that one of the functions of Sati is to calm your mind in preparation for the practice of Metta but before going on to practise Metta, there are a few things you need to know about it. As mentioned earlier, traditionally Sati and Metta meditations are practised together. This means that when you finish your Sati meditation, you will move seamlessly on to the practice of Metta. You will only be able to do that when you are familiar with the practice of both of them.

A reminder again, like anything you are not familiar with, when you begin practising Metta, it will be unfamiliar and feel awkward until you get the basic structure of the meditations memorised. If this is your first time meditating, it may take a few weeks to get familiar with it. Be patient with yourself and it will be worth it.

Metta meditation is unique in that it works on the emotional side of your being. To practise Metta, you will have to use a technique called visualisation. This is simple to do and, with a little practice and willingness, you will get the hang of it quickly. After a few weeks, you will be familiar enough with both the short Sati and Metta meditations to begin practising them together.

Individual Meditations

Although your ultimate goal will be to practise at least the short versions of the Sati and Metta meditations together, you can also practise them as separate meditations. However, they work best together even if you practise just five minutes of Sati followed by five minutes of Metta.

The practice of Metta affects how you relate to yourself and others and is a very powerful meditation. When it is practised after Sati, it is even more powerful.

What is Metta?

Metta is loosely defined as the practice of "loving kindness", in this approach the term "unconditional love" is also used. The reason for this is the term "unconditional love" may have a more familiar ring to it for some people. Either way in the context of this book it means the same thing. The practice of Metta is all about sending loving kindness or unconditional love to yourself first, your family, all your loved ones, your friends and beyond that, to the rest of the world.

The practice of Metta is really the "magic wand" of the world of meditation. If practised regularly and correctly, it will have a transformative effect on how you think and how you feel about yourself and others.

Metta, in Actual Practice

Metta meditation is normally practised in five five-minute blocks of time. Therefore, like the Sati meditation, a Metta meditation session will last for twenty-five minutes. These are not exact times; they are guidelines but do try to stick with them. It's very easy for a five-minute block of time to become six minutes. In actual practice, these meditations will last for about thirty minutes. The added time relates to the "preamble" or "transition time" between the Sati and Metta meditations and also the "warm down" time at the very end of your session.

Metta, the Process

During these five-minute blocks of time, you will be sending Metta (unconditional love) to five different categories of people. This means you will have to choose those people before you begin your meditation. This is very important! The following list is suggested to help you choose:

Yourself
An impartial person
A friend
A family member
Someone you dislike

A work colleague
An acquaintance
The whole world

You First

The first thing to take notice of on this list is that you are on the top. In all your Metta meditations, the first person to receive Metta from you will always be "you". This is absolutely essential because, if you do not give loving kindness to yourself, you will not have it to give or send to anyone else. Metta is all about sending and giving loving kindness but remember, you cannot give if you have nothing to give.

The next person whom you send loving kindness to will be an "impartial person", often called a "neutral person". This will be a person you know but do not have any kind of emotional or physical relationship with, other than you know the person and see them at some stage throughout your day. It may be the person you buy your groceries from. It could be the mailman or woman, a waiter or waitress or someone you meet when you are out walking.

The only other person on the list that might need a little explanation is "someone you dislike".

Someone You Dislike

Hopefully, there is no one on the planet you dislike, but just in case there is, the practice of Metta is one way you can alter this feeling. The word "dislike" does not really cover the depth of this subject matter but it is a gentler way of approaching what may be a more difficult feeling to deal with.

Disliking someone may be symptomatic of a far deeper feeling such as resentment. These can be a more serious obstruction to your mental, physical and spiritual health.

If so, it is essential for your peace of mind that they are removed.

Practising Metta, along with the three core steps is a very effective way to deal with resentments. You will need to be patient and compassionate with yourself when dealing with these concerns. Until you are confident in the practice of Metta, deal with the least troubling categories of people first.

Just Two

To introduce you to the practice of Metta meditation, you will learn how to send loving kindness to two people. These two people are first "yourself" then an "impartial person". When you can do this, you will be able to do the same thing with anyone else you want or need to send loving kindness to.

As you expand your capacity to send Metta to more people, you will soon be sending unconditional love to "the whole world". However, as already mentioned, before you can do this, you will first need to send Metta to "yourself".

It is essential to choose the people you are going to send Metta to before you begin. This is because it will ruin your meditation if you are trying to figure out who to send Metta to during the session. This may be a statement of the obvious nevertheless, it needs to be mentioned and adhered to.

You already know who the first person will be but you will also have to choose the "impartial person" before you start. Remember, it must be someone you have no emotional attachment to; you may not even know their name but you see them very often. One other thing during your meditation someone may pop into your head, if this happens by all means send Metta to this person along with those you have originally chosen. The most important thing to remember now is to choose who you are going to send Metta to before you start, always.

How to Metta Yourself

When you are practising Metta meditation, you will be doing a lot of visualisation. This is simply a way to see someone in your "mind's eye" so to speak. This may take a bit of practice to get used to but, it will be worth the effort. Metta practised sincerely, even if imperfect, will have a profound effect on all your relationships.

To begin a Metta Meditation on its own find a comfortable place to sit or lie. Close your eyes and do the preamble. Next send Metta to yourself. To do this visualise an image of yourself in your mind, sitting on a chair or lying on a couch or bed. See yourself happy and joyful in this image. Hold it in your mind for five minutes and repeat the following affirmation, pausing for five or six seconds between repetitions. Close your eye and try it now:

Metta Self

I send you unconditional love (Pause for five or six seconds and repeat the affirmation. Continue for five minutes)

Time: 5 minutes

How to Metta an Impartial Person

An "impartial person" is someone you know but have no emotional attachment to. It is important that there is no emotional attachment. It is equally important to choose the person before the meditation. Bring the image of the person to mind by visualising their face happy and joyful in front of you. Next say the affirmation. Close your eyes and try it now:

Metta Impartial Person

I send you unconditional love (Pause for five or six seconds and repeat affirmation. Continue for five minutes)

Time: 5 minutes

Remember all you have to do is continue repeating the same affirmation for five minutes pausing for five or six seconds between repetitions. Also while you are saying the affirmations you will be visualising an image of the person you are sending Metta to.

Practising Tips

Practise your Metta meditation using just these two categories of people every day for a number of weeks. This will take ten minutes, along with the preamble and a minute or two to settle into and come out of your meditation. The total time for your practice session will be fifteen minutes – the same as the Sati Meditation. As you become more familiar with both Sati and Metta meditations practise them together for maximum benefit.

As with the Sati meditation, to extend the Metta meditations, just add five-minute blocks. For your Sati practice sessions, you will be adding five-minute blocks of time, each with a different counting pattern. For your Metta sessions, you will be adding more people from the list of categories. Remember to use the same affirmation for all of them. Metta meditation is a powerful way to deal with old hurts and resentments but, be patient with yourself and use Metta on yourself often!

How Much Practice?

The amount of practice you do is entirely up to you but daily meditations are highly recommended. If you decide to practise daily, you will quickly begin to feel the benefits physically, mentally and emotionally.

However, it is probably best to start with very short daily meditations and gradually ease your way into it. If you try to do too much at first, you may end up doing nothing at all.

This meditation is adaptable and once you learn the technique, then you can basically improvise within the structure set out here. You can extend this particular meditation simply by adding additional five-minute blocks. For example, you may have loved ones or people you know who are sick that you might like to include in your meditations. To do this simply expand your Metta to include the people you would like to give loving kindness to.

About Mindfulness

Being mindful can only come about as a result of your own efforts. Be patient with yourself and remember, no one can do anything perfectly. Like anything else you do on the material plane of your existence, the best you can hope for is progress.

Although this book is not about mindfulness in the traditional sense yet, in another sense, it is all about mindfulness. This is why the practice of some form of mindfulness meditation is suggested for you, to add to your well-being maintenance toolkit. It is a powerful tool and can be used at any time, for any length of time, to further your development.

Turned Off

Many people are actually turned off meditation by the amount of time, they are told, they have to put into practising certain routines. Another turn off is the idea that you have to sit in impossible positions and postures to get any benefits. This is not so.

You will get the benefit of meditation with minimum practice and just getting the essentials right. This is, basically, doing what you can when you can. Doing just two minutes of Sati followed by two minutes of Metta meditation every day, along with the preamble would transform your life.

It is not the posture, the type of meditation or the length of time you meditate that provides the benefits. It is your willingness, sincerity and the regularity of your practice that will help keep you on the road to happiness and peace of mind.

The question is often asked, on the subject of meditation, as to what form of meditation is the best. The answer is, the one that you do. Just remember, it is better for you to do a five-minute meditation every day rather than doing five hours once a week. Commit to the minimum, do whatever you can beyond the minimum and you will be well rewarded.

Final Thoughts on Meditation

As mentioned earlier one of the mistakes made when people first start to practise meditation is to practise too much too quickly, then end up doing nothing at all. When you are new to meditation, practise a few minutes every day until it becomes a habit. Then continue this practice until it becomes something you really like doing.

In this way, you will quickly know if you want to take your meditation experience to the next level or just keep it at the maintenance level. If you approach it with this attitude, you will gradually allow the magic of meditation to come into your life and it will be more likely to stay.

As little as five minutes every day, along with the core steps and some of the other suggestions, will provide you with a powerful remedy for the stresses and strains of modern life. Time out, the Sati and Metta meditations introduced here are ideal for working on calming the mind and managing thoughts and feelings.

There is a lot to take in, in this chapter and it would be easy to get overwhelmed. Remember this is an approach to Mindfulness and Awareness Meditation designed to help you through the rest of your life so there's no hurry. Once you begin you will feel the benefits after that it's just a matter of enjoying the process.

The best way to approach these meditations is to gradually introduce them into your life. Unlike the exercises in the rest of this book where all of them can be learned in minutes and applied in seconds. The longer meditations in this chapter will take a bit longer to learn and to practise. However, even these can be condensed and learned in chunks and practised for as long as you want.

Think of the practice of The Core Steps, Time Out and the X Faculty as essential immediate requirements for your greater well-being. The others such as the long meditations are gradual acquirements but will greatly enhance your quality of life and help ensure your permanent peace of mind and contentment.

Mindfulness Meditations Outline

An outline of the Preamble, the Sati and Metta meditation practices is presented now as one long meditation for your convenience. Make a photocopy of it and place it alongside your timer during your sessions to help you remember the process until you have memorised it. It takes two minutes to do the Preamble, ten minutes for the Sati, ten minutes for the Metta and a few minutes to wake up (warm down). Total time 25 minutes.

Preamble:

I am aware of the sounds I hear outside. (15 seconds)

I am aware of the silence I hear outside. (15 seconds)

I am aware of the sounds I hear inside. (15 seconds)

I am aware of the silence I hear inside. (15 seconds)

I am aware of the chair supporting me. (15 seconds)

I am aware of my feet on the ground. (15 seconds)

Time: 2 minutes

Change the wording of the last two affirmations as needed:

I am aware of the bed (couch) supporting me.
I am aware of my body resting on the bed (couch).

Make sure you are comfortable before you go on. Move slowly if you have to move during your meditation to make yourself comfortable. Next go straight on and start practising your Sati Meditation.

Sati: Two Blocks of Time

Block 1

Say "one" in your mind as you "inhale", then "two" in your mind as you "inhale", next "three" in your mind as you "inhale" and so… to ten then go back to one and start counting again. Continue for five minutes.

Time: 5 minutes

Block 2

Say, "one" in your mind as you "exhale" then "two" in your mind as you "exhale" next "three" in your as you "exhale" and so on… to ten then go back to one and start counting again. Continue for five minutes.

Time: 5 minutes

Metta

To transition from the Sati to Metta become aware of and observe your breathing for one or two minutes. Next check the time then close your eyes and visualise an image of yourself as you are now, sitting on a chair or lying on a couch or bed. Hold that image in your mind then say and repeat to yourself the following affirmation. Pause for five or six seconds between each repetition. After five minutes move on to Metta the "impartial person" you have chosen. The total time for these two categories of people is ten minutes.

Metta Self

I give you unconditional love (Pause and repeat and continue for five minutes)

Time: 5 minutes

Metta Impartial Person

I give you unconditional love (Pause and repeat and continue for five minutes)

Time: 5 minutes

CHAPTER FIFTEEN

Addictions and Troubled Thinking

In the 1950s, medical and psychiatric associations in the USA began identifying alcoholism and other addictions as illnesses. The World Health Organisation also recognises these conditions as illnesses. This is important and relevant to this discussion because of the negative effects these conditions have on feelings, attitudes, thoughts and emotions. Also, alcoholism and addictions are not just illnesses of the mind but also affect the body and the spirit. They are subtle, dangerous and highly infectious.

Although alcoholism and drug addiction are the main discussion points, they are far from the only addictions identified by the governing health bodies. These illnesses will strip away your peace of mind, happiness and general well-being if you are close to any one of them.

Alcoholism and addictions are among the worst offenders when it comes to creating and nurturing troublesome thoughts and feelings. In this brief chapter, a number of important issues are raised and discussed in relation to these illnesses.

Types of Addiction

There are many types of addiction: drug, alcohol, gambling, work, love, food, sex, nicotine and even chocolate are among them. Alcoholism and drug addiction are generally acknowledged as the big two. This does not mean that the other addictions are less painful. In fact, all addictions carry the same prognosis, which basically amounts to death, insanity or get well. Whatever type of addiction you suffer from, these are the outcomes. Faced with these options, a sane person would choose to get well but unfortunately a lot of addicts will die or go insane.

Pandemics

Unfortunately at the time of writing humanity appears to be struggling through a stage similar to that of a very troubled adolescent. The COVID-19 pandemic, now raging in virtually every country across the globe, makes for a very unsettling worrying existence for many.

There is also another pandemic raging: that is addiction. There are very few people in the world who are not aware of someone who is affected by addiction, be it alcoholism, drug addiction or some other form of addiction. Just like COVID-19 you do not have to have the illness yourself to be affected by it.

If you have a loved one, a spouse, a close family member, a relative or a friend who is an active addict of any kind, this will hurt you badly. Addiction has the potential to destroy you and your loved ones: unless you know how to deal with it.

Subtle, Dangerous and Infectious

It was mentioned that alcoholism and addictions are subtle, dangerous and infectious. They are subtle in that an alcoholic or drug addict may not know they are addicts. Although they may know something is wrong, they may not be able to identify exactly what it is that's wrong. An addict in denial will never see the substance as a problem and, in a paradoxical way, this is correct because, for an addict, the substance is not the problem; it is the solution.

Addictions are dangerous in that they are takers and killers: they will take everything that the addict has and often, the last thing an addiction will take is the life of the addict. Not unlike the COVID-19 virus, in the worst-case scenario, it separates loved ones before it takes the life.

Addictions are infectious in that they behave in a similar way to a virus. The addict is infected before they know it. Then the infection is passed on to everyone who is connected with the addict. If there is a practising addict or alcoholic in a family, everyone in the family feels the effect, some more so than others. An addict may remain a-symptomatic for some time before the disease shows itself.

The true figures for the loss of life or, those who go insane as a direct result of alcoholism, drug addiction and addictions in general may never be known because of the stigma attached to these illnesses.

There is an Answer

The good news is that you live at a time in the history of human beings when addictions can be treated successfully. Therefore, if you want to get well, you can, but it is you who has to make the decision to get well.

The three core steps, along with the other suggestions presented here will help you to prepare for the rest of the steps that you will need to take to deal with an addiction. They will also help you to deal with some of the symptoms of addiction. So, if you know of someone who may be suffering with an addiction, you can introduce them to the three steps and this information.

Although the three steps, as presented here, will not be enough to deal effectively with an addiction, they will certainly help an addict find a solution if they want to.

Dangers and Negative Effects of Drugs

The negative effects of over-indulgence in alcohol and or other mood-altering drugs on feelings, attitudes, thoughts and emotions cannot be overstated. Although alcohol and drugs are usually separated in discussions and discourses relating to addictions, it is important to understand that alcohol is also a drug. Just because it is legal and socially acceptable does not mean that it is any less lethal than any of the other available drugs, legal or illegal. In fact, if the truth be known, alcohol is probably responsible for more deaths, injuries and misery than any other drug.

The Differences

Addictions are often mixed up and confused with other problems associated with drug and alcohol misuse. When this confusion happens, it is easy to mistake an alcohol or drug abuser for an alcoholic or drug addict. This needs to be corrected as there are a number of major differences. Some of these are summed up in an old saying, 'every alcoholic is a drunk but not every drunk is an alcoholic'. In the context of other drugs, this translates into, 'every drug addict is a drug user but, not every drug user is an addict'.

It is essential that you understand these differences so that you can recognise these illnesses if they show up in your life because, some alcohol and drug users are often mistaken for addicts. Remember, not every person who drinks alcohol will become an alcoholic and not every drug taker will become an addict.

Addictions like drug addiction and alcoholism are recognised illnesses and what's more, they are primary illnesses.

Addiction and Alcoholism

Addictions and alcoholism are primary deadly illnesses, which first affect the mental state of the person. This has a very negative effect on the thinking of a person and can lead to all kinds of mental problems. If this condition is not attended to, it will eventually affect the body and beyond that, the spirit of the individual.

By primary here is meant that addiction and alcoholism are not caused by the events of life. For example, sickness, death, divorce, poverty and depression do not cause alcoholism and drug addiction. It is actually the other way around. Addictions and alcoholism cause sickness, deaths, divorce, poverty and depression among other things.

Addiction

Addiction is a word mainly associated with the taking of illegal drugs and substances. It is also used in relation to gambling and food, for example, gambling addiction and food addiction.

Alcoholic is the term used to define a person who is addicted to alcohol. Alcohol addiction is sometimes used to describe the condition suffered by alcoholics but in the main, alcohol addiction is known as alcoholism.

What is an Addict?

An alcoholic or addict is a person who has lost control of the substance that they are using and cannot stop taking a particular street drug, prescription drug, alcohol or certain types of food, for example, chocolate.

The addict or alcoholic is totally dependent on their drug of choice and need it to survive. This means that they have to use this drug or they will become very ill and, in some cases, will die. As a result of this dependence, the addict and alcoholic will put themselves and others at great risk to get the cure or fix they need. Isolation, anger, fear, terror, loneliness, confusion and bewilderment are but some of the symptoms of addiction.

Addiction versus Recreational Drug Taking

Addiction is very different from someone who uses or abuses drugs and alcohol. The user or abuser uses drugs or alcohol for recreation and enjoyment but may never become addicted to the substance. The addict will be filled with terror, loneliness, shame, guilt and remorse every time they use. Alcoholics will often say, never again but within a short while, they will be drunk again.

The addict and alcoholic will often be aware of the hell they are going into but are powerless to stop. So called users and abusers of the same drug will be looking forward to the next trip or drunk. Drug and alcohol abusers may sometimes show the same symptoms as addicts and alcoholics. This is why they are often put together in the same category but, they are miles apart.

Twelve-Step Fellowships

Probably the most widely known and successful treatments available to care for addicts, alcoholics and all those affected by these illnesses are the many different twelve-step fellowships. Among them are Alcoholics Anonymous (AA or Al Anon), Food Addicts Anonymous (FAA), Gamblers Anonymous (GA), Narcotics Anonymous (NA) and Sex Addicts Anonymous (SAA).

Al Anon is an example of a twelve-step fellowship available for spouses and concerned persons of alcoholics. All these fellowships provide essential care for both the recovering addict or alcoholic and also, their families.

Treatment Programmes

There are also many drug-free treatment centres available for the treatment of addiction and alcoholism. These centres at least the successful ones generally base their treatment programmes on the twelve-step programmes mentioned above.

In a treatment centre, the addict or alcoholic is introduced to therapy, which will involve group and individual sessions. In some cases, a time in a detoxification unit may be needed before an addict or alcoholic can enter a drug-free treatment facility.

The period of time in one of these treatment centres varies and can be from thirty days or longer, after which time, the now recovering addict or alcoholic will participate in aftercare. After leaving a treatment centre, they will then usually continue with their recovery by becoming a member of one or more of the twelve-step fellowships.

Does Treatment Work

Yes, treatment works! The twelve-step fellowships have been tried and tested since the foundation of Alcoholics Anonymous in 1935 in the USA. They have been proven to be one of the best forms of treatment for recovering addicts and alcoholics. This recovery depends on the continuous practice of a twelve-step programme, if lifelong, contented recovery is to be maintained. The members of these anonymous groups and fellowships simply come together to share their experiences to help each other recover from the horrors of addiction and alcoholism.

Treatment Centres

Treatment centres also have a very good record and are an excellent way to kick start recovery. Probably the best way to ensure continued recovery is to combine the therapy of a treatment centre, including aftercare, with one or more of the twelve-step fellowships.

Any recovering addict or alcoholic who is willing to practise a twelve-step programme, to the best of their ability, will enjoy a full recovery from any addiction regardless of what it is and need never use a drug, drink alcohol or return to addictive behaviour again.

Prescription Drugs

Many people have to use prescription drugs. For some people, these drugs are absolutely necessary. Unfortunately, there are some people who overuse prescription drugs and become addicted. There are those too, who take prescription drugs that are prescribed for others.

One the dangers associated with prescription drugs is that some of them can be as addictive as some street drugs and can do great damage, unless taken as prescribed. Never, ever stop taking your prescription drugs without the advice of your doctor and never take prescription drugs prescribed for other people.

If you are using the three-step approach in this book, remember, it is always as well as and never instead of. The motto is, 'as well as and never instead of, except on the advice of your doctor'.

Reach Out

If you know of someone or, if you are experiencing difficulty around alcohol, drug taking or any other form of addiction, there is an answer. You can always reach out to any of the groups mentioned in this chapter. With the help of one or more of these groups, you will quickly learn how to deal with the troublesome, harmful and sometimes lethal consequences that accompany addictions.

It is very unlikely that you will be able to deal with a real addiction alone. If you feel that you need help in this area of your life, now is the time to make the change. You are not alone in this!

CHAPTER SIXTEEN

Stages of Progress

As you continue to make progress on your journey, you will go through many changes and stages along the way. These stages are actually stages of progress but sometimes they will feel like anything but progress. With most of the stages you won't even realise that you are going through them. On the other hand there are some you will definitely be aware of but once you know what's going on they are easily managed.

These stages can function as indicators as to where you are going and, where you are now. The thing about these indicators is that they can be a bit paradoxical. For example they may give the impression that you should be doing the opposite to what you are doing. Chapters 17, 18 and 19 will explore three of these stages.

In this chapter, you will find useful ideas on ways to observe yourself as you pass through some of the different stages of progress. This will help you to develop a sense of awareness in relation to your own existence in relation to where you are and where you want to be.

It is essential to be aware of your own existence because it is this awareness that makes you the observer of your own self. The more informed you are as the observer of your own feelings, attitudes, thoughts, emotions and behaviour the quicker you will move through the different stages of progress and awaken in the light of your spiritual self.

You Exist

The mere fact that you can think and speak means that you know and can at least say, "I exist." Writing back in the 17th century, the French philosopher, Descartes wrote, "I think therefore I am."

Every human being who has the ability to say and think these words is able to observe themselves. If Descartes is correct in his observation and you can think, then it is established, you exist. The fact that you can think and express what you think is even more evidence of your existence. Being able to think and express your thoughts and feelings are essential for your well-being.

There is no need to get into a major philosophical discussion about the complexities of existence. However, you do need to know and accept your own existence. You exist and this "you" is the observer and keeper of your mind and your body. What's more, this "you" exists independently of your body and your mind.

In other words, you are not your thoughts, your feelings or your mind. You are the observer of these faculties. You are the observer of your own faculties. You, as the observer are much closer to your true "self" – the existence that you are. Along with being able to think and feel, you can also "know". You can also make choices. This means that you are a thinking, feeling, emotional, living, breathing, moving, vibrating human – maybe even a spiritual being.

Movement and Motion

Nothing in the physical world is standing still everything is in a state of transition. Everything in existence is going through stages of growth or reduction, improvement or deterioration, getting stronger or weaker, better or worse, richer or poorer.

As a human being, you exist in a tangible physical condition and also in an intangible, psychological state of being. Together, these two make up your material existence.

As a material being on a material plane, you are vibrating, moving and in constant motion, even when you think you are not. For example, when you are sleeping, every atom in your body is vibrating, you are in motion and still progressing on life's journey.

As you are going through this part of the discussion, be aware that it is only your material existence that is being explored at this time. This is only a tiny part of what you really are. Your material being is but the seed or if you like the genesis of the magnificent being that you really are. As you go through the next few paragraphs, keep this in mind.

Life Cycle

The term "life cycle" is commonly used to mark the stages that a life form goes through, during the course of its life. It is also commonly used in the world of business, to observe the stages that a new product or business venture passes through during its lifetime. It is a useful tool and will serve to illustrate some of the stages of progress that will be negotiated on the way to peace of mind and contentment.

Everything in the material world is in a constant state of flux as it moves through its life cycle. This means that every material thing has to go through continuous transformation on its way towards fulfilling its own destiny. By observing material progress through the lens of a life cycle different stages of progress can be identified and planned for.

In your material human life cycle you will go through a number of identifiable stages as you go through your life. Being aware of this and where you are in your life cycle means that you will be better able to deal with the unknowns that show up in the different stages of your life.

Developing Faculties

When you consider human life, it becomes clear that material development is not just about your physical faculties. It also includes your mental faculties and probably many faculties that mankind has not yet acknowledged. One of these the X Faculty will be explored later. For the purpose of illustration, the human life cycle can be seen in the following table alongside the life cycle of a business.

Stages	Human Life Cycle	Business Life Cycle
1	Conception	Start-up
2	Birth	Introduction
3	Adolescence	Development
4	Maturity/Renewal	Maturation/Rebirth

During all the stages of your life cycle, you are in a constant state of development. For example while in the womb, you developed faculties for example, limbs, eyes and ears. Looking back from where you are now, it is easy to see that the time spent in the womb was a developmental stage in your material human life cycle.

As with every human being, your material human life began at the moment of conception. Nine months or so later, you were born and your life as an individual person began. Although you became an individual in your own right after you were born you were still dependent on other human beings for survival.

During those early years just like when you were in your mother's womb you were developing new faculties along with learning to use those you developed while in your mother's womb. For example you learned to walk, talk and listen making use of the faculties you developed while in the womb.

You were also developing life skills for use in the next stage of your life cycle, which is adolescence. This pattern continues throughout out your material existence. A more detailed discussion on this and related topics can be found in *Some Answered Questions* by Abdul Baha.

Following this line of thought you can see that in each stage of your existence you develop the faculties you will need when you reach the next stage of your existence. If for example you did not develop the organs you need to hear and speak when you were in your mother's womb you would be at a big disadvantage when you were born into the next stage of your existence. Conception, Birth, Adolescence and Maturity are fundamental stages in the life cycle of every human being.

Cycle of Stages

Looking at your life as a cycle of stages is a way of getting an overall picture of your material self and your journey through life. It offers you a lens through which you can observe your progress. This will help you stay aware of where you are at on your journey, where you have come from and where you are going. It is a way of making sense of and dealing with some of the more challenging stages in your life.

Some people will pass through the stages of their life cycle with great ease and may not even be aware they are doing so. Others will feel every bump on the road. Yet, every human being has the capacity to recognise the stage of life they are in when they have the use of reason. At that stage you are able to choose a way of living that leads to peace of mind and happiness or one that leads to misery. When you have the ability to distinguish what is good for you from what is bad for you your well-being becomes a matter of choice.

The choices you make will affect your feelings, attitudes, thinking and emotions (FATE). The choices you make in relation to your FATE are responsible for how happy and peaceful you will be as you go through your life cycle. This means that you have the ability to choose and change your own fate.

How Many Stages?

The number of stages you go through, as you continue to grow and develop in your life, will differ for each individual. In reality, there can be any number of stages. Writers and commentators have identified a variety of stages. For example, the life cycle of a business idea or product could have four stages as mentioned earlier: start-up, introduction, development, maturation.

As you saw on the life cycle table, a business idea or product life cycle looks remarkably similar to the life cycle of a living organism. This is not an accident because the life cycle of organisms, human or otherwise, is the model generally used to represent a life cycle. History has provided many theories and models on the different stages an individual may go through, as they journey through the stages of their life.

Models and Theories

There are many models and theories that attempt to mark the stages that you can pass through on your journey in life. As with the four-stage life cycle of a human being presented in previous paragraphs they offer other and different ways of viewing and trying to make sense of human life.

For example, one of Carl Jung's representative models of the stages of development in the life of a human being suggests two stages "morning" and "afternoon". The morning being the first stage and earlier years of life and the afternoon being the second stage and the latter years.

These two stages are not seen as being equal in length but, according to the theory, when life is being lived to the full, the morning ends and the afternoon begins. Under normal circumstances morning ends around the mid-thirties and the afternoon begins. This will vary if the mind of the person is troubled.

In each of these two stages, the mindset is different. This theory suggests that an individual cannot live a fulfilling "afternoon" of life with the same mindset as was present in the "morning" of life. As you make your way through the stages of life, your mindset has to change and adapt.

There are many other models and theories. Some have put the number of stages that you may go through at two, some four, some seven or more.

Trick of the Mind

Unfortunately, many people tend to opt for the scenic route when it comes to their peace of mind and wellbeing. If you choose this option, you will spend most of your precious time stuck in some stage of your life trying to deal with emotional and spiritual pain of one kind or another.

Sadly, during these times, some people will lose their minds and others will even lose their lives. However, this will only happen if you allow your mind to trick you into thinking it is in charge. Some people are so deceived they allow their mind to take full control and run completely wild. They live their lives out of a head full of troublesome thoughts and a heart full of hurt feelings.

This need not be you. If you are willing to accept that "you" are in charge of your own feelings, attitudes, thoughts and emotions (FATE) then you will thrive using the approach set out in these pages. This will bring changes and challenges into your life, that's for sure, but that's what life is all about; changing and adapting as you grow and develop.

Remember it is not the strongest or fittest people who survive and prosper but those who are willing to adapt to the changes and challenges of life. You have the power to manage your FATE but it will manage you if you let it. This is a simple fact of life.

Change and Challenge

Change is something that challenges everyone; once you accept this fact, you are already a winner.

It is said, by many, that change is the only constant in the material world. Yet, when the challenge of change comes calling, the alarm bells go off. When the unfamiliar starts to happen, many people will immediately think that they are going the wrong way and start turning around.

Change should not be feared, it is something that needs to be embraced if you are to live a full life. It is an illusion to think anything in life stays the same. Everything is constantly changing and moving.

Becoming comfortable with change, ambiguity and uncertainty is a quality that needs to be cultivated as you grow through the stages in your life. This will allow you to live in the present, free you from the unnecessary fear of the unknown and allow you to live in peace and harmony with the world around you, at all stages of your life.

Experiences and Changes

As you continue to practise this approach to well-being, you will experience many changes. Some, you will be aware of immediately and others will be more subtle. In whatever way you experience these changes, keep in mind that they are all indicators that you are on the move and making progress.

Some experiences and changes in the stages of your life will be marked by denial, fear and despair. At other times, the stages will be marked by experiences and feelings of peace, happiness and well-being. Awareness of what you might encounter, on your way through the stages of your life, will help make your change experiences not just more manageable but also enjoyable.

Many people go through their life unburdened. They seem to have been born with a natural ability to let go and enjoy the journey. Others go through life as if it were a living hell. This need not continue. It is possible for you to make the necessary changes to improve your live, no matter how terrible it appears to be right now.

In the following brief chapters, denial, anger and despair are explored and explained as stages of progress.

Chapter Seventeen

Denial

When you begin to move or change in any way, the first thing that you will encounter is resistance. In relation to the management of thoughts and feelings, one of the ways that resistance shows up is in the form of "denial". It is not the only way resistance shows up but it is central to this discussion because it will be a part of your progress. It is the first of the three stages of progress to be discussed.

Denial is often the first response to any attempt at change. Before you begin to practise the steps and start to change, denial is present but it hides itself so well that it allows the person in denial to lie to themselves sometimes for years and sometimes, for a whole lifetime. It is only after you become aware that you are changing that denial becomes noticeable and needs to be dealt with.

This and the other two stages of progress are common to all and therefore, when you start to grow and develop, you will experience them as your journey progresses. They are contradictory in that when you first experience them, they appear to be suggesting that something is wrong but in actual fact they are a sign that something is right and a sign of progress.

Response and Defence

How you respond to and defend yourself against the traumatic experiences in your life may not be as unique to you as you might think. Human responses to really bad news for example, a sudden death in the family, a car crash, serious illness or other traumatic events tend to follow a pattern. That is to say, the human brain reacts in a fairly predictable way. This response is a reaction and defence mechanism and will involve denial, anger and despair.

For example, if you or any of your loved ones are experiencing extreme stress, depression, anxiety, loneliness, grief, isolation, etc, their response and defence and yours will include different levels of denial, anger and despair. These are among the primary natural responses and defences against the traumatic events in the life of every human being.

Denial

Denial can be as simple as a refusal to accept what life has just thrown at you. It may be a feeling, an attitude, a thought, an emotion that basically says, "No. I refuse to accept this."

It is this lack of acceptance and in some cases, the refusal to even acknowledge that something is wrong that makes dealing with denial complicated. Denial can be even more extreme and persistent and can cause a person to completely refuse to accept anything at all connected with the realities of life.

When you are more familiar with the practice of this approach, you will be able to see denial as a sign that something is changing that needs to change. At this point, the three core steps of the approach can be used to name, share and let go of denial once it is identified and acknowledged. Remember, your mind will still want to be in charge. It does not respond well to being changed and denial is one of the ways it keeps things as they are. It likes the 'same ole, same ole' and will usually try to resist any attempt to change the status quo. Denial is a sign that it is time to change but only you can implement that change.

Coping Mechanism

Denial is a coping mechanism and as such, is used when a person does not want to deal with or does not know how to deal with certain troublesome feelings, attitudes, thoughts or emotions around a situation. For example, when very shocking news has been heard, – the sudden death of a loved one, the loss of a home or job – denial will prevent a person from dealing immediately with the trauma involved.

In cases where there is a lack of communication or in extreme cases, no communication at all, denial will find a place to settle and can be very difficult to shift. Therefore the quicker you can identify it the quicker you can let it go.

Identifying Denial

Denial is not all negative although it may often be seen as such. In reality it is simply a coping mechanism and an essential form of self-preservation. It can be difficult to identify denial because it shows up in all sorts of ways.

For example, blaming others, not wanting to own one's part in situations, not willing to look at certain behaviours, not taking responsibility for actions are among the many ways denial tries to conceal itself. Denial is a common response to life's more painful experiences and is generally neither a good nor a bad thing, unless it is ignored!

Difficult to Deal With

Although, in this chapter denial is being dealt with as a stage of progress nevertheless it is also a feeling, an attitude and an emotion and can therefore be dealt with as such. It is true some people deal with the unpleasant things in life without difficulty. It is also true that others need a bit more encouragement before they can return to feeling well and happy again.

If a person stays in denial, the feelings and emotions around some of the more challenging things in life may never be dealt with. Unfortunately, this can allow troublesome thoughts and feelings to take up a permanent residence in your life. You now have the tools to deal with them but you have to use these tools.

It is best to deal with denial the moment you identify it but this applies to any of life's troublesome thoughts and feelings. No matter how trivial you think a problem may be, if it bothers you deal with it as quickly as possible; name it, share it, replace it.

In most cases, people are intuitively aware that they need to deal with their painful "stuff" but, this can be very difficult if you do not know how. Moving beyond denial starts when you decide you want peace of mind and are willing to do whatever it takes to get there.

Removing and Replacing Denial

To remove and replace denial, begin with the three steps and practise affirmations continuously. Remember this involves applying the three steps as they are written. As mentioned earlier the reason for doing the steps exactly as written here is that the words you use are crucial to the result you achieve.

Your mind will accept the words you use if you say them often enough. Therefore you need to know exactly what words to use. That is why you should stick to the script until you know exactly what you are doing. To let go of denial fill in the blanks but do not write on the book instead, use a blank sheet of paper and a pen:

Name it: *I am in denial about_____ I now let go of my denial.*

Share it: *I am in denial about_____ I now let go of my denial.*

Replace it: *I accept my own thoughts and feelings. I am free of denial.*

The Denial Stage

Remember denial becomes obvious when you are faced with a sudden, traumatic situation, such as the death of a loved one or the diagnosis of a serious illness for you or a loved one. The first response will more often than not be something like, "No! Not now! I don't want this."

Denial is not something to be feared. It is simply one of the stages and tests that you will pass through on your journey to peace of mind and happiness. The good news is that for most people, it will just be a bump on the road. For others, it will be like a fork in the road and you will have to make a decision as to which road to take.

Sometimes denial can be hard to identify but, like all feelings, attitudes, thoughts and emotions, the more you practise, the easier it becomes. The practice of the steps and the other suggestions will give you a perfect vantage point to observe and deal with whatever you experience. If you become aware that you are holding on to denial, use the three steps to deal with it immediately. This will allow you to move quickly through this stage of your journey.

Chapter Eighteen

Anger

Another stage of progress you are likely to encounter on your journey is anger. While you are in the denial stage, anger is kept at bay by the fact that whatever you are in denial about will not be on you radar. Sooner or later, it will show up in your life and you will no longer be able to ignore the obvious. This is when anger comes into the range of your radar screen and you will know it's there. At this point, denial is replaced by anger and where there is anger, there is stress, anxiety, fear and frustration.

Anger is unusual in that it is like one side of a coin that has fear on the other. This means that anger and fear go side by side. Where one goes the other goes too. This dualism can make anger tricky to identify. This causes problems when you are trying to manage anger and fear because one can often be masquerading as the other. Sometimes anger is just a front for fear and this makes it difficult to name specifically.

Progress

As with all the stages you go through on your journey when you arrive at the stage of anger it is a sign of progress. This is because this anger only becomes noticeable after you are finish with denial. This brings with it the realisation that the troublesome feelings, attitudes, thoughts and emotions that were ever present in your life are in the process of being removed and replaced. This can bring a sense of bereavement into your life leaving you feeling angry, afraid and relieved.

This type of anger is unfamiliar because it is not the kind that is acted out in random emotional outbursts for no good reason. On the contrary, anger from this perspective is a real sign of progress. This, however, does not mean that you will not be troubled by this anger. It just means that you are now more aware of it and your other feelings, and crucially, you are now more aware than ever of your progress. This stage of your progress if understood and acted on will also provide additional encouragement and support for you to keep going.

Remember!

Identifying and acknowledging are two of the fundamental parts of naming and dealing with troublesome thoughts and feelings. Ultimately, denial, anger and despair are no more than troublesome feelings, attitudes, thoughts and emotions and therefore, can be managed using the steps. They are also stages of progress you will go through as you journey from the world of worry, stress, fear, anxiety and misery to lasting peace of mind and contentment.

Denial, anger and despair are also forms of self-deception. This is particularly true when it comes to matters you may not want to deal with. The good news is that these stages can now be identified and named without too much bother because now you know what they are and how to deal with them. This means you can quickly pass through these stages and say goodbye to this kind of anger, denial and despair along with any other tests you may encounter on your way.

How quickly they go depends only on how willing you are to let them go. There may be a tendency, at times, to remain in some stages a bit longer than is necessary. This is usually because of the fear of the unknown and the fear of change. However, you will eventually have no choice but to go on or go back. Given that there are no troublesome thoughts and feelings that you want to go back to, the only real option you have is to move forward, towards peace and happiness.

Letting Go of Anger

It was mentioned earlier that anger has a kind of dual personality and because of this, it can be tricky to deal with. This is because anger and fear will sometimes hide behind one another. This can make them very difficult to deal with because to let anger and fear go you must be specific about what you are dealing with.

When practising step one, you will be trying to identify the feeling you are letting go of specifically. This is because the more specific you are, the more successful you will be. Therefore, you will need to be able to identify anger for what it is. The same applies when dealing with fear.

Being specific applies whether you are dealing with a feeling of fear, an attitude of intolerance, a thought of suicide or an emotional outburst of anger. This is because you cannot let go of something unless you have it, then to let it go you must name it, but you can't name it until you identify it specifically. The more specific you are, the more successful you will be.

Any time you experience anger, it is a good idea to ask yourself, "Am I afraid?" If the answer is yes, then apply the steps to the feeling of fear.

Removing and Replacing Anger

In the following example of the steps you can name and share feelings of anger and replace them with peace of mind and calm. Remember, before you can replace a thought or feeling, you must first let go of the old feeling. It will not work any other way. You can then move beyond anger, by replacing it in step three:

Name it: *I feel angry because I have to change. I now let go of this anger.*
Share it: *I feel angry because I have to change. I now let go of this anger.*
Replace it: *I embrace change I have peace of mind at all times.* Repeat!

Don't forget! Repeat the affirmation a number of times pausing for a few seconds between repetitions and keep sharing!

Quality or Trait

Anger, like fear, is one of those essential feelings and emotions that can be an enormous benefit, or hugely destructive if not managed.

Whether anger or fear is a quality or trait depends on what causes it and the intention behind it. If your anger is born out of an attempt to do what is right for example in the promotion and defence of fairness then it can be considered a human asset or quality.

On the other hand, if the source of your anger is selfishness and self-centredness then it is a human liability or trait and it is going to be very destructive for all in your circle. Human traits and liabilities will ultimately lead to misery and unhappiness for you and your loved ones.

You Have the Answer

Anger gets a lot of bad press but anger is not all bad because as just mentioned it can also be a quality. Regardless of what it is, it still has to be managed because if you don't manage anger, it will surely manage you. Of course, this is true of all feelings, attitudes, thoughts and emotions, so when it comes down to it, they all have to be managed.

How deep-rooted the anger has been allowed to get will often be a determining factor in how quickly you can remove it from your life. However, it really does not matter how embedded a trait is, it can be removed and removed quickly if you are willing to do what it takes. With the three steps and other suggestions you need never be a prisoner to any kind of troublesome thoughts and feelings again.

Blink

Like all troublesome thoughts and feelings, anger can be managed and removed in the blink of an eye. This depends entirely on you and on how much you want it removed. Sometimes people get attached to their thoughts and feelings and do not want to let them go. This can definitely be a difficult obstacle to overcome however it's just a matter of choice.

One of the difficulties with anger is that some people get satisfaction from acting out on their anger. This makes it difficult to let go of simply because you may be getting satisfaction from it, even though it may be destroying your life and the lives of your loved ones. This can make anger addictive and if so, it may need professional intervention or a specific form of therapy, such as an anger management course.

The longer it is left unattended, the more damage it can do. Therefore, the quicker the willingness can be found the quicker you will pass through the anger stage of progress and on to the next.

Brothers

It was mentioned earlier that anger is closely related to fear. In fact, they are so closely related that they may even be twin brothers. Most of the time, anger is just a front for fear. There is an old saying, "Show me an angry person and I will show you a frightened person."

Furthermore, fear is not an only child; it has many siblings. For example, where there is anger there is fear, anxiety and stress and, not too far away at the extreme end of the fear spectrum, you will find terror. Some, if not all of these feelings will be encountered as you move through the different stages of progress. They will need to be dealt with, so that your journey towards peace and happiness will not be delayed.

Fortunately, all the feelings associated with anger and any others that you encounter along the way can be dealt with by applying the three steps. For these changes to be permanent, you should also practise as many of the other suggestions as possible. The important thing, for now, is to keep practising the three steps.

Dealing with Stress

As mentioned earlier stress is closely related to anger and therefore needs to be dealt with in this stage as well. To deal with stress or fear related feelings you don't really need to know what caused it or why you are stressed out. What matters is that you know how to let it go. If you find out why later that's ok but for now just let it go.

If you are stressed out by family situations, mealtimes or work situations you do not have time to be analysing why you feel the way you do. The likelihood is that you already know anyway. Therefore, what you need to be able to do is let go on the move.

When you are practising the steps most of the time you will not have someone to share with near you. That's ok share with yourself until you find someone to share with. Also don't forget the helplines! To let go of stress use the steps as follows:

> **Name it**: *I feel stressed out. I now let go of this stress.*
> **Share it**: *I feel stressed out. I now let go of this stress.*
> **Replace it**: *I am calm and relaxed under all conditions.* Repeat!

Remember when doing step three, you can repeat the affirmation a number of times, pausing for a few seconds between repetitions. Since you are doing the steps in this example on the move you may not be able to be as specific as you could be. If so, you can explore the idea of being more specific about the stress later. For example, when you name it, you can be more specific and say what you are stressed out about. Likewise when you are sharing be more specific as to what you are stressed out about if you can.

Repeat the whole process as often as it takes. Keep it all very simple and try to avoid analysing yourself. Don't forget to keep using the Time Out exercise which is also a tool to help keep stress and tension under control during a busy day.

Anxiety

Anxiety is another feeling that is closely related to the anger that you may encounter during this stage of progress. Anxiety is a word many people are all too familiar with, especially in these days of the COVID-19 pandemic. Even without the lockdown, most people will have experienced some form of anxiety at some time in their lives. Although the feeling of anxiety can be very distressing, it can actually be dealt with very simply by using the three steps as follows:

Name it: *I feel anxious about the COVID-19 virus. I now let go of this anxiety.*
Share it: *I feel anxious about the COVID-19 virus. I now let go of this anxiety.*
Replace it: *I am peaceful and relaxed under all conditions.* Repeat!

Don't forget when doing step three, you can repeat the affirmation any number of times pausing for a few seconds between repetitions. Also a quick reminder; sharing is the heart and the engine of the three steps and needs to be carried out as soon as you can after naming it.

Beyond Fear

Although this part of the discussion is about anger as a stage of progress and it is important not to lose sight of this, the fact remains that anger, in any form, is closely related to fear in any form. Therefore, it can be dealt with in the same way as any other feeling or emotion.

Of the many feelings closely associated with anger, stress and anxiety have been singled out because on some level they will affect everyone who sets out on the road to happiness and peace of mind.

There are a few others but just one more will be mentioned for now. This one is at the extreme end of fear and is called terror. Even the sight of this word on the page can cause people to become anxious but, like any other feeling, it can be dealt with easily. Use the steps as follows:

Name it: *I am terrified of_____ I am now letting go of this feeling.*

Share it: *I am terrified of_____ I am now letting go of this feeling.*

Replace it: *I am safe and secure at all times and under all conditions.* Repeat!

Again when doing step three, repeat the affirmation a number of times, pausing for a few seconds between repetitions. Also remember to share, share, share.

The Importance of Sharing

As you continue on your journey, naming, sharing and replacing as you go you will find that these anxieties, fears and worries that used to ruin your life are gradually and sometimes instantly losing their power over you. The importance of sharing will become increasingly clear, especially as you move through the stages of progress. Sharing is the heart of the steps and the seed of lasting fellowship. This is why having the right person or persons to share with is so important.

For example, when you are sharing troublesome thoughts and feelings, it is good to share with someone who won't try to fix you. The reason for this is that no matter how well-intentioned the person is, they can't fix you. This is something you have to do for yourself.

There are many great people out there who will be willing to work with you on this approach to well-being. What you need to do, as soon as possible, is to find someone to share with, who is empathetic and who is able to just listen. Remember, if you have difficulty finding such a person, don't forget you can always use the helplines. They are confidential and free.

You are aware, by now, that to manage stress, anxiety and terror effectively, one of the most important things you can do for yourself is to share it. However, sharing will have little effect if you don't know what you are sharing. This means that you can't share it until you name it and beyond that, you can't replace it until you share it and let it go. Therefore, to manage these and other troublesome thoughts and feelings the three steps must be used together.

One other thing you need to know about fear, stress, anxiety and the like is that everyone will have to deal with these throughout their life on some level. Some people won't even know they have these feelings. Either way remember, it's ok to have these feelings but it is not ok to let them ruin your life so, name, share and replace them.

The Anger Stage: The Conflict is Over

The Anger stage of your journey, like Denial, is another one of the tests you will experience at some level as your journey continues. However, going through the stages is not something to be feared. All stages can be crossed easily using the steps and the other suggestions.

The Anger stage is sometimes referred to as a time of internal conflict. It is a time of knowing that you have to let go of the old ways of living and replace them with the new. The conflict arises from an attachment to feelings, attitudes, thoughts and emotions and behaviours that you know you must let go if you are to have the life that you want. This is what produces the conflict and it is part of the grieving process that you will experience as a result of this perceived loss.

Also, as you move from battling with the events and situations in your life to a more composed and peaceful way of living, you will, from time to time, fall into the old way of doing things. This is to be expected but when it happens, you must get back on your feet as quickly as possible and continue on your journey.

This will actually be one of the main differences between the old and the new you. In the old way of living, if you fell, the likelihood is that you may have stayed down a while longer, from now on, your response to a fall is to get up as quickly as possible and continue your journey.

The best and quickest way to end internal conflict at this stage of the journey is to use the power of surrender. Say, "I surrender. No more conflict for me."

This has the paradoxical effect of allowing you to walk away from conflict and anger.

The Steps and Other Suggestions

By now, you will be aware that the journey towards greater well-being is definitely about managing feelings, attitudes, thoughts and emotions. To achieve this, you will need to be practising these suggestions daily. If you have been doing this correctly for a while, you will also know by now that they work, how they work and they are absolutely essential.

Furthermore, you are now aware that this approach is non-intrusive in your life. You can gradually introduce the ideas and exercises without too much interference. The reason for this is that virtually every exercise in these pages can be applied in seconds and will last for the rest of your life if you use them. Keep in mind also that no real progress will be made, unless you cultivate the willingness to change and let go of all the old attitudes that didn't work for you.

If you are still unsure as to how the three steps work, this is a good time to go back and review Chapter 2 and go over them again quickly, just to make sure that you are getting the idea. There have been many examples given throughout this book on how to use them but a quick read through Chapter 2 will help keep you on your toes.

Remember the three steps are essential. They are like a door into the world of transformation. It's time now to move on to the next stage of progress.

CHAPTER NINETEEN

Despair

No doubt you have heard it said, "the darkest hour is just before the dawn."

In your darkest hour, it can be difficult to see any hope or any way forward. This is especially so when dealing with thoughts and feelings, despite the fact that you are actually about to experience the light of a new day.

When the darkest hour comes, it is likely that you may feel some if not all of the following: powerless, hopeless, frightened, alone and isolated. What this amounts to is a feeling of despair. As you read this, you may be thinking to yourself, "I want none of this thank you very much."

Hang in there because you are about to make a major breakthrough on your journey but remember, you must be willing to keep going. In other words, you must be willing to keep practising the steps and any other exercises or suggestions that keep you on the road.

This chapter too is all about the power of surrender and the wisdom of paradoxes. Here, you will learn more about these tools and how to use them. As you continue, keep in mind that it takes only seconds to apply these tools although, it will take a bit longer to understand why and how they work. You are just a moment away from a major breakthrough in your life.

Almost Home

During this stage of your journey, you are actually closer than you have ever been to a major transformation in your life. Again, this is one of those paradoxes that keep cropping up as you navigate your way towards your destiny. It can sometimes feel like the end but this is actually just the beginning.

This stage is marked by certain characteristics, which are simply thoughts and feelings that need to be managed. Remember, despair itself is really only a feeling but for you to be able to manage it effectively it needs to be explored a little bit more.

During this stage, you may experience some, if not all of the following: confused, beaten, friendless, helpless, stressed, worried and hopeless. Whether you feel any or all of these feelings depends largely on how far down the scale you have been in your own life. However, regardless of how far down you have gone, you will find your way to peace of mind, if that is what you really want in your life.

The reason why troublesome thoughts and feelings just mentioned, show up at this time, is because your mind wants to hold on to control over you and it starts to play tricks. You may also feel like you do not want to continue on your journey. Your mind may tell you to go back. It may tell you that you are going the wrong way. This can be very confusing. However, all this can be seen as a big signpost on your journey, telling you to keep going you are almost home.

Confusion

It is easy to get confused at this stage on your journey. Sometimes, it can feel like you have arrived at spaghetti junction during rush hour traffic, with no idea where to turn. There seems to be uncertainty everywhere. This simply means you need to take action. First, tell your mind to stop!

Now, here's the thing! If you tell your mind to "stop" when it starts to unravel and confuse you, it will do so. You may need to do this a few times but as you gain more control over your thoughts and feelings, you will get results. If you are alone, do this forcefully and say it aloud. Reminder the word "stop" was mentioned earlier in relation to dealing with panic and, it's a real power word.

Beaten

You may feel like you can't go on and that you are completely beaten but, you struggle on you fight the good fight. However, it is not until you know and accept that you are beaten that you will reach your destination. When you are able to accept that you are beaten you are the winner of the fight with life. Not alone will you win but you will have arrived at your destination and the doors to peace of mind and happiness will open up before you.

This means you have to stop fighting with life and accept that this struggle will not bring you happiness. This may not be easy for some but it is simple for everyone. Unfortunately, some will continue looking for conflict but this need not be you. The fight with life is fought again and again by human beings and it will continue until someone says enough. When dealing with life's material and emotional conflicts the only way to win is to disengage and surrender. In other words, stop fighting with life and you will become the beaten winner.

I Surrender

Surrender is mentioned quite a few times throughout this book. The reason for this is that this concept is essential for your continued progress. It is one of the indispensable human qualities that you will need for long term peace of mind. Therefore, "I surrender, the fight is over for me" is an affirmation that should never be far from your lips. The idea of surrendering in the context of managing thoughts and feelings is known as a paradox. In this sense it simply means doing the opposite of what is expected to get a desired result. For example, to win certain conflicts you must accept defeat and surrender.

You have probably heard it said that sometimes "the fighting continues long after the war is over." This is mainly because human beings are very slow to stop fighting. So, wars are fought and people suffer and die to satisfy the whim of other human beings who think they know more than you. The death and destruction that's left is then interpreted, in some way, as being a victory for one side or the other. There are no winners in war. According to the Tao, when war ends the victor should celebrate by mourning.

Yet, it is from the words of war that the best defence against a marauding mind comes. For whatever reason, troublesome thoughts and feelings are always ready for conflict. One of the best ways to manage them is not to engage with them. This does not mean you ignore them you've got to name them, share them and replace them. If you are already in conflict the best way to deal with them is to surrender:

Say, "I surrender, the conflict is over for me." Repeat!

Use this affirmation often as an independent exercise.

Helplessness and Hopelessness

Despair is generally associated with helplessness and hopelessness. In the context of the solution to managing troublesome thoughts and feelings, this is not so. From now on, these words take on an entirely new meaning and you will understand these words and others like them on a deeper level. For you, this can be the end of the old way of thinking and the beginning of the new.

As you move forward, your understanding is not limited to literal meanings of any words. For example, when you are going through the stage of despair, it does not mean that you are helpless or hopeless. It means the opposite. This is another paradox. You are now closer than ever to your goal of peace of mind and happiness.

So, although despair and the feelings associated with it can seem frightening when first encountered, you can now go forward with confidence, knowing that you have the tools to deal with any situation with which you are faced.

Powerlessness

You are about to open a door and enter a new stage in your life. To open this door, you will need to make use of yet another paradox. This one relates to powerlessness. The wisdom of the past shows that powerlessness is really the highest point of human understanding.

One of the reasons for this is that when you acknowledge and accept your powerlessness, you will be setting everything in your being to zero. This is the same as emptying yourself and resetting everything. What actually happens when you acknowledge and accept powerlessness all internal conflict ends and you begin to experience mental clarity and freedom. Beyond acknowledging powerlessness acceptance will allow you to hold on to the clarity and freedom for as long as your acceptance lasts.

If you practise powerlessness every day you will experience more and more peace of mind. To practise powerlessness you can use the three steps on it every day:

Name it: *I am powerless and dependent.*
Share it: *I am powerless and dependent.*
Replace it: *I now allow wisdom and understanding to enter my life.* Repeat.

Acknowledging powerlessness in this way has a paradoxical effect. It means that once you acknowledge and accept powerlessness you can then allow it to be replaced by wisdom and understanding. When you have reached this stage of your progress you will be letting go of the limiting feelings, attitudes, thoughts and emotions that have kept you back. They will be replaced, naturally, with wisdom and understanding in proportion to your practice and willingness to let go of your old ideas.

Conscious and Unconscious Thoughts

Thoughts come to the human mind at every moment in life. Generally speaking, you do not control why, when and what thoughts come into your mind. Your mind is like a big, magnetised sponge that just sucks in anything within range. Your mind loves information and thoughts and feelings are full of information much of which is inaccurate.

Unfortunately, the mind cannot tell the difference between useful information and informative junk so, it takes it all in and eventually gets clogged up. When this happens, it needs to be unclogged and although you will not be able to stop your mind from taking in all this information, you do have the power to let it go.

This means you will have to catch your thoughts and hold them before you let them go. When you do this, you must avoid engaging in conflict with them because if you do, you will lose. Therefore, since you cannot stop thoughts from coming in, you will have to know how to let them out again. The three core steps – name it, share it, replace it are designed for this purpose. Keep in mind, thoughts come and go if you let them.

Loneliness and Despair

Loneliness, of one form or another, is never too far away from any stage of this journey but there is a particular kind of loneliness associated with despair. It should not be confused with being alone or the loneliness a person feels during the course of normal living.

In the course of a lifetime, most people will experience some form of loneliness but this does not last. It is quickly relieved by going for a coffee with a friend or meeting with a family member or loved one.

This is because people are social beings and generally thrive on company and social interactions. Unfortunately, social interaction is not really an option during these days of COVID-19. Be that as it may, this kind of loneliness can be managed using the three steps.

Social Contact Not Enough

Social contact, drugs and alcohol will not be able to help you come out of this kind of loneliness. Social contact is, without doubt, something that every human being needs. It will certainly help to relieve the kind of loneliness brought about by the COVID-19 pandemic. However social contact alone will not be enough when dealing with the more troubling thoughts and feelings associated with the stages of progress.

If you are blessed enough to have someone in your social circle who can identify with this loneliness you are already halfway there. The people who experience this and come through it can really help others come through it as well. Sharing your experiences with those who know what you are talking about can be a real game changer in this situation but it needs more.

COVID-19

At the time of writing, nearly every country in the world has had to introduce some form of social distancing as a result of the COVID-19 (Coronavirus) pandemic. Social distancing involves individuals and households having to physically distance themselves from family members, other loved ones, neighbours and friends. Sometimes, people have to isolate from family members in their own homes.

Some will take this in their stride but others will have great difficulty as in some cases it involves complete isolation from family and loved ones. The variance in the way people react to the situation is because every person is unique and different.

The practice of the three steps, and the other suggestions during and after the pandemic, will help you deal with any troublesome thoughts and feelings that you experience as a result of the lockdown experience. The final chapters in this book will also explore a new way of looking at your own existence in relation to the world as you know it right now.

Stages and Experiences

As you continue to practise the steps and the other suggestions, you will begin to experience more changes taking place. You will also begin to experience your own development on a different level. This progression will, in the course of your life, take you through many more stages of progress. Many of these stages will be common to all but some will be specific to you. Some will be your own personal experiences and these will later become your greatest assets.

Remember, it is in the sharing of your experiences that you will clear the way and allow great benefits to come into your life. This holds through in all three stages. As the sharing and listening part of the experience develops, conversations around feelings, attitudes, thoughts and emotions will get deeper and you will leave the most painful parts of your life behind. Remember if you are having difficulty finding someone to share with, you can always use the helplines until the right person comes along. Sharing is absolutely essential!

The Passing of Despair

As with all thoughts and feelings associated with the stages of progress, despair can also be removed and replaced instantly using the steps. After all, it is just a realisation that the old way is gone and it is time to replace it with something new that works. Once you have named and shared your feelings of despair, replace it with affirmations.

You are being reminded of the three steps again and again so that you will realise how important they are to your happiness and peace of mind. Despair will pass and turn to joy, and you will know a life of contentment. Everything passes and you will move on to the next stage of your journey, whatever that might be but remember, you have to be willing to try.

Material or Spiritual

Despair marks the end of the material part of your journey and the beginning of the spiritual. Of course you do not have to develop your spirituality that is a matter of choice. If you choose the material path only it will continue to benefit you but, it won't guarantee your peace of mind in the long term. On the other hand, if you choose the spiritual path, you most definitely will be stacking the cards in your favour.

Why not have them both? What if you are both a material being and a spiritual being at the same time. What if French philosopher, Pierre Teilhard de Chardin was right when he suggested that a human being is a "spiritual being having a human experience."

In the next chapter, you will be introduced to one of the faculties that really makes you special in the world of being – the X Faculty.

Chapter Twenty

The X Faculty

As you practise this approach to well-being and grow through the stages of progress, you will begin to see changes in your life. These changes will be evidenced in the way you feel, your attitude, your thinking and your emotional responses to the situations you face each day. If you continue to practise, you will continue to change and develop.

However, as powerful as the three steps and the other suggestions are, they will only work on the material level of your being. This means that the steps and all the exercises affect only your psychological and physiological condition.

In other words, they only work on your mind and your body. If you consider yourself to be just a mind and a body, then this may be as far as you want to go. However, if you want happiness, contentment and peace of mind to be the mainstay of your being then you will need to continue your journey.

In this chapter, you will discover different and probably new ways for you to observe and see yourself as a human being.

Other Faculties

The more you are able to manage your thoughts and feelings, the more your mind will clear and you will become aware of other possibilities beyond your purely material existence. Consider the possibility that you may have other faculties. There is no denying the benefits of a sound mind and body but to deny the possibility of other faculties would be very unwise, if not downright foolish. If you want your life to improve continually, you must be open to all possibilities otherwise, you will be depriving yourself of the fullness of life.

You are now about to explore the possibility that you have faculties that you have not yet used, at least consciously. Let's say, you have at least one other faculty at your disposal and this is called the X Faculty. You probably have many more but for now, the focus is on this one.

Information and Your Mind

It is probably acceptable to most people that human beings have a mind and a body with a brain. This mind is completely dependent on a fully functioning brain if it is to function effectively. You have a brain and a mind otherwise, you would not be conscious and able to read these words.

Your mind is supplied by much of the information it receives through the activity of the brain. Much of this information comes through your body by way of your senses. However, your body and your senses are not the only sources of information your mind can draw on.

Your mind also receives information that's not coming through your senses. For example when you are unconscious or asleep your mind is still receiving information in the form of ideas, inspiration and dreams. This information is not coming through your senses because your senses are in sleep mode but it has to come from somewhere. Maybe other faculties? The flow of this information does not stop when you are awake the ideas, inspiration and dreams continue to flow.

Sleeping and Mental Activity

It is not just your mental faculties that are sustained when you are asleep; your hair continues to grow and essential bodily functions such as your heart and lungs are also maintained, without the need for you to be conscious. When your body and mind are in sleep mode, something keeps them functioning and you continue to have feelings, attitudes, thoughts and emotions, sometimes troublesome and sometimes happy and peaceful.

If your body and brain are asleep and if they were the only source of thoughts and other information, then there would be no activity in your brain or in your mind and no peaceful dreams or nightmares to disturb your sleep. It would appear that information of some kind or other is coming from at least one other source. Now, at this point, you and perhaps many experts will say that when you are asleep, information is simply being supplied by the subconscious mind. That may be so but, what if there are other sources of information and faculties that are being ignored?

The End of the Subconscious Mind

What if there was another way of looking at your mind? For example, instead of looking at the human mind as if it were "conscious" and "subconscious or unconscious", what if there were no subconscious mind? What if what has been called the subconscious mind, up until now, is simply another faculty? What if you could use this faculty for your benefit? Then you wouldn't have to be afraid and concerned about what might be buried in this so-called subconscious mind.

Remember, the concept of the subconscious mind is simply part of a theory that tries to explain how the human mind is constructed and works. What you are being asked to consider now is the possibility that you do not have a subconscious mind at all, just another faculty. What you are presented with is simply another way of looking at your mind and also, the possibility of other faculties you may possess.

If you decide to accept the view that you may not have a subconscious mind but instead, have one or even more other faculties at your disposal, then everything changes. You will have faculties at your disposal that you can use to bring great changes into your life. One reason for this is that you will no longer be a prisoner to the so called "subconscious" mind.

The X Faculty

For the purpose of this discussion, instead of seeing your mind as being conscious and subconscious, you are asked to try and see it as a multifaceted unit with no hidden compartments. This means you will need to replace the so-called subconscious mind with another faculty. Let's call this other faculty the X Faculty.

When you do this, everything changes because now, you will be able to see yourself and all you can potentially become. This is because up until now, your so-called subconscious mind, supposedly filled with suppressed thoughts, feelings and memories, has kept you prisoner. You now have the key to this prison.

There are three very important features to remember about the concept of the X Faculty at this point. First it is separate from your mind. Second, it does not depend on either the mind, the brain or the body. Third, it functions as a store house and conductor of information and other data to the brain, mind and body.

When you start to use the X Faculty consciously, you will quickly start to distinguish what is real and beneficial from what is unreal and of no consequence. You will be able to identify what you need to let go of and what you need to hold on to. You will be able to name and share troublesome feelings, attitudes, thoughts and emotions and let them go immediately. In addition you will have opened a channel that allows wisdom and understanding to flow into your life. Qualities such as wisdom and understanding are the same as spiritual assets and qualities.

Your Spiritual Essence

If you decide to take on this way of looking at how your mind works you will be transformed. First you will see that you are more than just a body, a brain and mind. It's as if you have two sides or a twin personality. During the remainder of this discussion, these sides are referred to as the material and spiritual.

Next you will be able to conduct an inventory of your spiritual assets using the emotional stocktaking exercise in Chapter 6. To do this simply change emotional assets to spiritual assets and emotional liabilities to spiritual liabilities and complete the inventory as it is. Your spiritual assets are a measure of your actual happiness. The more spiritual assets you have the more peace and contentment you will have.

You will come to accept that generally speaking your feelings, attitudes, thoughts and emotions are just pieces of information that highlight the behavioural choices you make in your life. You can choose to ignore them or act on them. The main point to remember about thoughts and feelings is that they will come and go if you let them.

Beyond that you may even come to realise that you are indeed as Pierre Teilhard de Chardin wrote a "spiritual being having a human experience."

Spiritual Guidance System

The X Faculty acts as a kind of a conductor of information, in the form of memories, spiritual feelings, comprehensions and awareness, to and from your material self to your spiritual self. It also acts as a kind of spiritual guidance system, in that it transmits what is best described as spiritual information to your mind but, it is in your mind that you make the decisions about what to do with this information.

At this point, it gets complicated because your mind is also receiving sensory information through your brain. Consequently, this can result in internal conflict. When a decision is made in your mind, you, the person, will activate this spiritual guidance system and discard or act on the decision, based on your own values and standards.

How you act and behave in relation to these decisions has a direct effect on your happiness and well-being. Remember, you have complete control over your actions and behaviour in relation to your own values and moral standards.

Many Other Faculties?

The X Faculty can be an expression of many other faculties and capacities that you have available, to assist you on your journey through this world. It can be seen as a channel that connects your mind with your spirituality or even your soul. Some may see it as a connection with their Angels and Saints. Some may even see it as a connection with the Prophets, the Messengers and Manifestations of God.

Whatever the X Faculty turns out to be for you, it is the heart and soul of this approach to managing thoughts and feelings. Without it nothing happens because even though the three steps, the meditations and the other suggestions in this book work really well if they are practised, they will not sustain peace of mind and happiness in the long run.

The X Faculty is essential for the permanent maintenance of both the spiritual and material side of your nature. Without this faculty your peace of mind won't last. If you can accept that you are more than a body with a brain and a mind, then you will be able to start developing your spirit. Ultimately, it is the neglect and denial of the spiritual nature that creates all the unhappiness in the life of human beings.

When you start to acknowledge and use your X Faculty you will quickly arrive at a door into another world. This other world is the land of your spirit and the home of your soul. If you decide to accept this perspective and go through this door, you will begin to experience a kind of material and spiritual transformation that you could only have dreamed of.

Use Your X Faculty

Like all of your other faculties, if they are not used, they will become dormant. In this the X Faculty is no different, it needs to be used otherwise it will remain lifeless, hidden and undeveloped. Knowing that something exists is one thing, using it is another. The question is, how do you use it?

What if the X Faculty can be seen to act a bit like your brain? Remember your brain uses your five physical senses; seeing, hearing, tasting, smelling, touching, to collect information and send it to your mind and throughout your body. Is it too much of a stretch to see that a faculty such as the X Faculty is somehow connected to the source of a spiritual version of your senses? For example: instinct, ideas, memories, thoughts, creativity, feelings and who knows what else.

What if you could make use of these senses, let's call them spiritual senses. Instead of having this subconscious mind that cannot be used for any other purpose other than create confusion in the area of mental health you would now have a faculty you can use to your advantage. Would this not be a step forward for humanity in the quest for peace of mind and happiness?

In much the same way as you can intentionally make use of your brain when you are working on a project, reading a book or writing an e-mail you can also consciously make use of your X Faculty for example when you are trying to remember a name or come up with new ideas. No doubt, you have heard the saying, "use your brain" well now it's time to "use your X Faculty".

Conscious, Accessible, Knowledgeable

For the X Faculty to be useful it must be a provider and or source of useful information. It must be conscious, accessible and knowledgeable. It cannot be an unconscious source because the information you receive is intentional in that it is often in response to your efforts or a request by you. It must be easily accessible and it must have access to intelligent sources of information or problem-solving abilities. It needs to be identifiable. Otherwise it would simply be another version of the so-called subconscious mind.

Although other sources of information have been referred to as the faculties of the soul it really does not matter what you call them. They will still be the same thing but they have to be called something. What matters is that you know that when you use your X Faculty, information from your soul, your essence or your inner being in the form of instinct, thoughts, ideas, memories, awareness, silence, sound, all kinds of creativity and information flows back and forth between your inner being and your mind.

Just like what happens between your brain and your mind the flow of information between your inner being and your mind sometimes happens automatically for example when you are asleep. It also happens when you are awake for example, when you are being creative or trying to memorise or remember something.

A Channel for Information

One way to view the X Faculty is as a facilitator of the flow of information from your soul or inner being to be acted on in your mind. Your inner being or soul by extension would have to consist in part of other facilities which include your ability to communicate, comprehend, memorise, imagine, think, be creative, and love among other things. These could just as well be called the faculties of the soul.

Therefore the X Faculty can act as a channel for information sent by your soul to your mind, in much the same way as your brain can be seen as a conductor of information to your mind from your body and your senses. Decisions are then made in your mind based on the information received.

In your mind, you decide what kind of life you are going to have by the actions you take as a result of the decisions you make. It follows then that since it is in the mind decisions are made that effect how you feel it is in your mind you decide how and if you are going to be happy or sad. Your mind can also be seen as being like a bridge between the tangible material world and the intangible spiritual world.

Not Just a Bridge

But your mind is not just a bridge. As just mentioned, it is also the receiver and processor of the information that comes from both your material existence and your spiritual existence. This makes it a complex junction, dealing with numerous endless roads full of vehicles, with all kinds of information. Your mind is wonderful both in its simplicity and its complexity but it needs concrete information to make correct decisions.

Generally speaking concrete information flows to your mind from the outer material world of your being, by way of your senses through your brain. Information also flows from the inner world of your being facilitated by means of your X Faculty. When you use this faculty, you will also be using your mind to process and express the choice of behaviour or action you will take depending on the information you receive. This means that in your mind you will assimilate the information presented to it and then decide how you will act.

The behaviour and actions that follow will be based on your own values and standards. Acting or behaving outside your own values will leave you feeling unhappy and miserable. On the other hand if you act within your own standards and values, you will find happiness and peace of mind all the days of your life. If you make the right decisions and act within your own values and standards consistently you will not slip back into morbid thinking or allow troublesome thoughts and feelings to re assert themselves in your life.

Intentional Use

There will be times when you use the X Faculty intentionally and there will be times when you use it intuitively. When you are using the X Faculty intentionally, you will also be using your mind but remember, your mind is a busy junction and there will always be traffic, in the form of thoughts and feelings, running through it. To be able to use of your mind for maximum benefit, you will need to know how to empty it instantly. The practice of Time Out is designed specifically for this purpose.

You are intentionally using the X Faculty when, for example, you are trying to remember the name of a place or the name of a person you haven't met for a long time. In this instance, the information that is the name will come from your memory, which comes through the X Faculty, from your soul. Remember the soul is where memories are stored. You use the X Faculty to locate the memory and bring it to your mind. When the information is in your mind the decision is made as to whether it is correct or otherwise.

Any time you put the X Faculty to use on the material level of your being, you will be doing so using your mind. Remember the intentional decisions and choices you make are what will ultimately bring happiness or sadness into your life and these decisions are made in your mind.

Intuitive Use

The intuitive use of the X Faculty could happen, let's say, as in the example in the previous paragraph, where you could not decide on the name of the person immediately. Then, a couple of hours or days later, maybe you are out walking and suddenly the name pops into your mind seemingly from nowhere. For this to happen, the information must come from somewhere and since it hasn't come from the tangible, material part of your being – that is through your senses – it stands to reason that it came from somewhere else.

The view put forward in this book is that the somewhere else is not a "subconscious mind" but your "inner being" or your "soul". Of courses the senses can also be involved but on their own they cannot provide the answer.

You can make more effective, intuitive use of the X Faculty through the practice and cultivation of your spiritual assets for example kindness, compassion and unconditional love. Use the three core steps to remove undesirable spiritual liabilities and replace them with spiritual assets using the power of affirmations. For example, to affirm the spiritual asset of patience in your life use step one and two to name and share the spiritual liability of intolerance then:

Replace it: I am patient in all areas of my life.

Repeat the affirmation often and remember to pause briefly between repetitions.

Keep in mind as you go on reading that what is being suggested and described here is just another way to see yourself as a human being. It simply suggests that there are no secret rooms or cupboards in your mind filled with frightening skeletons and ghosts from your past waiting to jump out and sabotage your life at every twist and turn.

Helping Yourself and Others

Every human being has an X Faculty unfortunately most people have been educated into the idea that they have a subconscious mind. Human beings have the ability to tap into and use the X Faculty consciously but all use it unwittingly. They may not call it the X Faculty but that is what it is, at least until another name is found for it. Unfortunately, the full benefit of this faculty cannot be realised until it is consciously acknowledged and used.

There are people who will get some benefit from the X Faculty, mainly because they haven't fully bought into the idea of the unknown, mythical, subconscious mind. Unfortunately, most have accepted it. Some have been so damaged by often well-intentioned people that, they are left with no solution to the emotional turmoil they have to endure. Yet, many of these difficulties can be removed by just being willing to acknowledge that there may be another point of view.

You are one of the lucky ones to have found this approach and now, along with continuing your own progress, you will also be able to help others deal with their troublesome thoughts and feelings. Of course, you can only help others after you have helped yourself and if they want to be helped. Unfortunately, some people do not want to change.

You Can Be Happy

Sadly, some people have convinced themselves that they cannot be helped. in other words they cannot be happy and peaceful and they have accepted misery as their lot. You have the power to take control of your own wellbeing if you are willing to do whatever it takes.

No matter how bad you feel, you can change and live a full life again. Although your mind may resist and try to keep you where you are, you have the power to change your mind and enjoy a happy and peaceful life.

Say, *I can change. I am changing.*

Repeat often as part of the three steps or on its own. If you are willing to do whatever it takes to have peace and contentment in your life then you will have it. Never forget the power of your own words. When it comes to bringing change into your life there is no power greater than the power of your own words. When used correctly, as in the three core steps and suitable affirmations, that power is multiplied.

Your Mind Depends on Your Brain

Remember, unlike your mind, the X Faculty and your Soul do not need your brain. Your mind, unaided, will not be able to cope with life for long because of the complexity of the feelings, attitudes, thoughts, emotions and other matters it has to deal with. Your mind is a magnificent facility but, it needs the support of a healthy brain. It also needs information, some of which comes from the physical senses. The information that your mind receives from the senses needs to be correct; otherwise, the decisions that it makes will be wrong or at least questionable.

Your mind gets its sustenance from your body and your brain. It also gets support from the X Faculty, your soul and your inner being. The human mind is a dependent faculty. It needs a body, a brain and other faculties to be able to function. These are just some of what it needs and if it is deprived of these, it will not function properly in fact it may not survive at all. It is completely dependent on other faculties.

This makes your mind very fragile unless you are aware that you have other more powerful faculties you can call on such as the X Faculty, your Soul and your Inner Being. To have peace, happiness and well-being, the human mind needs to be taken care of because even though it is powerful it is also fragile. It is complex but paradoxically it is also simple. It can be trained in that it will accept whatever "you" train it to accept. This of course means that you are not your mind "you" are something much more.

Your Mind Is Not Alone

As you can see your mind is not alone and it cannot exist without your body and your brain on the material side of life. These are not its only supports. Along with supplying information collected by the senses to the brain, your body also provides life and energy, through the other essential organs. This means that when you are trying to improve your overall well-being you must also take care of your body. Of course your body is not the only support your mind has. Unfortunately, many people have been educated to believe that all you have is a body with a mind. This makes for unimaginable loneliness and isolation for some people.

The X Faculty also supports the mind but unlike the concept of the subconscious mind it does not need the mind or the body. It is not dependent on either the body, the mind or the brain. The X Faculty is an essential extension of your inner being. It will continue working with or without the body and the brain. For example, consider what occurs when a person is found to have failing brain cells as in the case of an illness like Alzheimer's.

Alzheimer's

This particular illness can cause such symptoms as memory loss, mood swings, changes in behaviour and effects the ability to communicate effectively, among other things. These symptoms are all as a result of brain cells that are malfunctioning and therefore, are affecting the mind. This is because the mind is totally dependent on the brain for its material existence. The X Faculty, on the other hand, is not dependent on the brain and therefore is not affected.

For instance, people with Alzheimer's respond remarkably well to songs and music. The view put forward here is that the X Faculty is still providing the feelings, attitudes, thoughts, emotions and the memory, hence the response to songs and music. However, because the brain cells can no longer provide the information the mind needs to make basic decisions, the mind cannot do so. This can leave the patient frustrated, confused and disoriented. The mind is the decision maker in relation to material existence. Remember your material existence covers both your physiological and psychological makeup.

The X Faculty does not get confused; it does not need information; it is a provider of information. It operates like a channel through which information flows on its way to your mind. Unfortunately, in the case of Alzheimer's the mind can no longer function properly because of the damage to brain cells. Thus the patient is limited in what it receives from the senses through the brain nevertheless the mind continues to receive information from the soul through the X Faculty.

This example illustrates the dependency of the mind on the body and the brain. It also shows that just because a person cannot communicate through speech or the other standard ways as a result of injury to the brain it does not mean they cannot communicate in some other way. It just means that a different language is needed for example the language of music. This example also points to the probable existence of other human faculties one of which is for now called the X Faculty. Obviously, this whole area needs further research!

Your Mind and You

Here are a few ideas and possibilities for you to reflect on about your mind. You need not fear your mind. Your mind is not the boss. You are not your mind. Your mind uses your intellectual faculties. You use your mind; don't let your mind use you. Your mind has plenty of support; it is not alone. Your mind needs information to draw conclusions and make decisions.

Your mind is dependent on your body. Your mind is dependent on a healthy brain. You are your mind's minder. Your mind thinks it knows. A big difference between your mind and the X Faculty is that the mind "thinks", the X faculty "knows".

The X faculty is an unbreakable link between the tangible material world of places and things and the intangible spiritual world of creativity, the arts, the sciences and spirituality.

Intangible

One of the difficulties, when it comes to acknowledging such concepts as the X faculty, is that it is, in itself, intangible. However, it is no more intangible than the subconscious mind. Although this intangibility means it cannot be seen or touched in the physical sense, you can tell that it is there by its effects. These effects include the creative arts, sciences and the human and material qualities evident in humanity.

Due to the intangible nature of the X Faculty, human beings tend to ignore or deny its existence but it is there and as clear as the light of the sun to those who make use of it. Therefore, it should be investigated by each individual before making a judgement otherwise you will remain forever in ignorance of it.

If it weren't so serious, it would be quite funny because the relationship between the physical body and the X Faculty can be likened to what happens in the ring at the circus. You know that part of the circus where the ring master is looking for the circus clown, who is standing right behind him. Like anything intangible, nobody really knows what or where it is but everybody knows it's there.

How do they know? The answer is because of its effects. Take your mind, for example. You have never seen it but you know it's there. How? Because of its effects.

The Baby and the Bath Water

There are many schools of thought within the field of psychology. According to some of these the subconscious mind is a very powerful part of your makeup. Some will tell you it records everything that has happened in your life. It is also said that your subconscious mind can have a profound impact on your life.

Now that you have replaced or, are in the process of replacing the idea of the subconscious mind with the X Faculty, it is important not to "throw the baby out with the bath water."

Some of the descriptions applied to the subconscious mind by the schools of thought within Psychology fit much better on the X Faculty. Unfortunately, this does not give the full picture and many, instead of investigating concepts such as the X Faculty further, prefer to hang on to an idea that offers very little by way of direction or hope to those who are the seekers of happiness, peace of mind and greater well-being.

More Faculties

The main take away, from this chapter, is that if you want peace and happiness to be a constant in your life, you will need to start seeing yourself as much more than a body with a brain. You have additional faculties available to you to help you live a more fulfilling life.

You have a faculty called the X Faculty available right now. It will enable you to transform your life for good if you are willing to learn about it and use it.

All the academic education or so-called intelligence in the world cannot take the place of such faculties. The X Faculty is the gateway to wisdom. You also have other faculties that you will also become aware of once you begin using the X Faculty. These faculties actually make you the individual that you are. However, the only way that you can fully benefit from them is through your own efforts, your own choices. For more detailed discussions on some of the topics in this chapter check out: *Closer Than Your Life Vein* by Henry A. Weil.

When it comes to managing your feelings, attitudes, thoughts and your emotions which is just another name for your FATE, you have complete jurisdiction. You are the captain of your own FATE-ship and you can decide to sail the seas of life or paddle in a pond and watch the world go by.

CHAPTER TWENTY-ONE

Spirituality

In this chapter, the concept of spirituality is explored. This subject will be reasonably familiar to some people but for others, it will be completely new. For some people, spirituality will involve some form of religious belief and for others, it will have nothing at all to do with religion. This part of the discussion will explore what spirituality means in the context of this approach to well-being. It will help you become aware of your own spiritual needs and what you can do to have those needs satisfied.

Becoming aware of your own spiritual needs and direction is essential to your well-being. It is especially so now as humanity approaches what hopefully are the end times of its adolescence. This means that as some degree of maturity is achieved each individual must take more and more responsibility for their own well-being. Developing your spirituality is essential if you are to be able to sail your FATE-ship to peace and contentment.

As the old political, religious and economic systems collapse under the weight of their own inability to solve the problems of the times, new and wonderful systems are already in the making. If you want to have peace of mind and happiness in these times, then you will have to take the responsibility of examining your own spirituality and investigating new ways to live. Cultivating a spiritual way of living is one sure way to transform your life for good.

Social Media, Fake News and Spin Doctors

In this world of technological advancement and the onslaught of social media platforms, you can no longer allow others to decide your material or spiritual fate. You cannot rely on social media, regardless of its source for any reliable information because, sadly, "fake news" has become the norm.

Furthermore and unfortunately, humanity is also in the grip of the spin doctors, whose sole purpose in life appears to be to distort every piece of information and turn it into a version of what they think you should hear. Therefore, you must now investigate all things for yourself, whether its religious, political or economic.

The practice of the three steps and other suggestions will allow you to clear your head enough to allow you to quickly make progress in your quest. If you are sincere, you will be drawn to what is right for you. Within a short space of time, you will be able to distinguish what's true from what's false, no matter where you hear it.

This part of your journey will take you to the next stage of your spiritual existence. It will involve being open-minded and willing to listen to different points of view as you search for what is true. Remember every human being is on the same journey but all at different stages. The suggestions put forward here will give you some idea of what you may experience as you continue your journey.

Spiritual Language

When you open up to the world of spirituality, you will discover things known only to those who already walk the spiritual path. What you discover can only be communicated by the spiritually minded, not just in words but in many other ways too. For example, a smile, a nod of the head, a tear in an eye, a wave of the hand or a simple hello are among the many ways of spiritual communication. However, it is not just the gesture but the quality and intention that holds the message.

This kind of communication is part of the language of the heart, which is spoken fluently only by those who are spiritually awake. As you awaken spiritually, you too will begin to speak the language of the heart and be able recognise others who are also spiritually awake. In addition you will begin to attract others who are themselves on the spiritual path.

More Paradoxes

You will also come across many more paradoxes and sometimes, logic will appear to have been abandoned completely. However, if you stick with it, you will begin to get a better understanding of what it means to be spiritual. You are about to enter a world where you will discover that your human spirit is your connection to numerous other faculties and resources that are available to you. Unfortunately, many people remain unaware of these faculties and never get the benefit of using them. They remain deprived of what it means to be a truly spiritual being. You will learn to tap into your spirit, so that you can become more aware of your own potential.

Open-Minded

When you consider anything that was ever made by a human being, be it a table, a chair even a jumbo jet, it has all come about as a result of a thought. This thought then becomes a design and finally, a reality. However, it takes someone with an open mind, who is willing and ready to acknowledge the thought, to turn that thought into a design and finally, turn that design into a reality.

This is what happens on the material plain of existence and illustrates how something is conceived and brought into existence as a result of open-mindedness. If you are open-minded, everything is possible. If you are willing to search for answers and investigate the validity of what you are presented with before passing a judgement, you will succeed in all of your endeavours.

Spiritual Exploration

One of the many ways of looking at spirituality is that it is a way of being and thinking about yourself, your relationship with people and with the world that you live in. Of course, there are many ways of looking at this mega topic and you will discover many of these for yourself as you grow and develop. However, since you are reading this, you are, at least, interested in exploring the concept of spirituality a bit further.

Here are some questions for you to ponder. What if you are a spiritual being with a mind, a body and an intellect? What if, as was mentioned earlier, French philosopher, Pierre Teilhard de Chardin was right and you are a "spiritual being having a human experience"? What if you are not just an intelligent animal? What if you have a spirit and a soul? What is a spiritual being? What if you have been ignoring the greatest resource available to you?

What is Spirituality?

For the purpose of this discussion, spirituality is seen as a state of being that exists independently of materiality. In some ways, spirituality is dependent on the material side of existence to develop and grow. This is only in so far as it is through making the correct moral choices and acting on them that spiritual development is facilitated.

For example, if you choose to have an attitude of intolerance and constantly act out on it, you will not have peace in your life. On the other hand, if you practise kindness and tolerance in your life, peace and happiness will always be yours. This is spirituality in action and is a sign of spiritual strength.

Spirituality is not about being perfect, it is about being willing to live an ethical life, based on values, and a willingness to develop ethical human qualities. You may not always succeed in keeping these standards. Being spiritual means that you will fall, but it also means that when you fall, you will get back up and try again. Spirituality is the surest way to achieve peace of mind and happiness and maintain it.

Spiritual Beings

A spiritual being will have some defining qualities and characteristics. Among them are humility, compassion, the ability to reflect, to know right from wrong, to possess understanding, to know what acceptable and unacceptable behaviour in a community is, to have the ability to make moral choices.

These are some of the defining characteristics of spiritual beings and indicate that human beings are at least capable of living a life, which is on a different level than all other creatures on the planet. Human beings can make choices. Other creatures are compelled, by nature, to live the way they live. This shows that human beings have other faculties and perhaps, other natures.

Animals, Plants and Minerals

Where does animal, plant and mineral life fit into this picture? They too have a spirituality but this spirituality is restricted. Look at it this way. Human beings, relative to animals, plants and minerals, are on higher level of existence. In the world of the animal, there is a certain freedom but relative to human beings, this freedom is very limited.

For instance, animals are compelled by nature to live the way they live. This gives animals a certain kind of perfection in that they can do no wrong. There is no good or bad, right or wrong in the world of the animal. They do not have to make choices in the same way that human beings do.

More specifically, they cannot make moral choices, which is one of the essential characteristics that make human beings what they are. The level of existence enjoyed by plants and minerals is also relatively restricted but, as in the world of the animal, they too enjoy their own level of perfection.

A Matter of Choice

Making the correct moral choices in your daily affairs will make you happy. The choices you make directly impact the way you feel. This means that if you are a physically and mentally fit human being with the capacity to be honest, the moral choices you make in your life will have a direct effect on how you feel.

Furthermore, the choices that you make are actually shaping your fate. This means that in every choice you make, in relation to your attitude, actions and behaviour, you are deciding your FATE as to whether you are going to be sad, anxious, depressed, miserable, happy, peaceful or joyful.

Since human beings have complete freedom in relation to their feelings, attitude, thoughts and emotions and the freedom to discard their spiritual nature, this makes them responsible for their own happiness and peace of mind. So, as you see, happiness and peace of mind are ultimately a matter of choice.

Atoms and the Sun

Everything in the known universe is moving and vibrating. If you have ever had a conversation with a Reiki practitioner, they will tell you that everything is, vibrating and in some way, energised by some kind of life force or power.

If you ask an atomic scientist about the nature of atoms, they will tell you that atoms of one kind or another are at the core of everything in the material world and they are in a constant state of vibration or motion. They have a power within them far greater than anything a human being can imagine.

This power is released when atoms are split. It is the splitting of atoms that has the effect of causing an "atomic explosion". The explosions created from the splitting of atoms is so powerful that it has been likened to the sun. This is because it is similar to what takes place in the sun, as it generates the power and energy to sustain life on the earth.

Power

Minerals, plants, animals and human beings too are all energised and kept alive by the power of the sun. In this sense, every material thing in this solar system is connected and dependent on each other. As powerful as the sun is, it is only one of uncountable billions of stars in the galaxy of the Milky Way. In turn, the Milky Way is one of uncountable billions of galaxies in the universe, all in some magical way, connected to each other by an unseen power.

This power is known because of its effect. Everything is in existence as a result of this power. Every movement is as a result of this power. For example, the coming together of atoms, which are attracted to each other as if in a preordained way. The planets travel around the sun without any human intervention. All human beings have to do is sit back and enjoy the views and the spin.

Universal Power

There is no denying that the solar system is set out in a particular way. It appears to be carefully designed and managed by powers far greater than can be imagined by any human being. As powerful as the sun is and all the other stars, they too appear to be part of a greater system or design, held together by some kind of unimaginable power.

It is obvious to the wise that as amazing and powerful as the universe is, it too appears to have a designer and creator. There can be no serious denial that there exists a power capable of bringing billions of stars and planets into being, not to mention the other forms of life that exist across the vastness of the universe. This cannot be denied realistically.

Human beings who are awake spiritually know this to be true because they experience it in every moment of their life. Whatever this power is, it provides the life-giving energy that keeps the universe working as one.

Unfortunately, history has shown human beings have gone to war to promote or condemn this power. Some have even made it their sole occupation to try to get rid of this power, or place limitations on it. There have been many names given to this power over time but in this book, this power is called God.

Spirituality and Spiritual Beings

Every spiritual person is a human being who is willing to walk the spiritual path but, not every human being is willing. You will know a spiritual being by their attitude, their behaviour and most of all, by their countenance.

Spiritual is what you are, in other words, you are a spiritual being and this can be seen in what you do. Your level of real spirituality will be seen in your actions and by how you manage your feelings, attitudes, thoughts and emotions.

Your spirituality is not necessarily connected to a religion or a belief system. It can be but religion per se is not what makes a person spiritual. However, although some spiritually minded people may prefer to keep themselves separate from "religion", this does not change the fact that all of the moral standards and laws, practised all over the world, have their basis in religion of one form or another.

Remember, it is the moral choices you make and practise that allow you to have happiness and peace of mind and, live the life of a spiritual being. Considering where these standards and laws come from, it may be best not to discard religion altogether. This can be hard to take for some but it would be a pity to "throw the baby out with the bathwater" after coming so far on the spiritual journey.

You will eventually come to know and understand what it means to be spiritually awake but this insight will only come through your own personal efforts and willingness to change. Your attitude and behaviour and the moral choices you make will be the true markers when it comes to your spirituality.

Either Or

To grow and develop as a human being, it is necessary to shift your thinking away from the "either or" world of, for example, the idea of nature or nurture. In psychology, it is accepted that human development and behaviour is influenced by both nature and nurture, not one or the other. Nature and nurture can be seen as independent of each other but both are essential for human development.

Of course, there are those who believe that if it is in your genes, you cannot change it. That may or may not be so. This discussion is not going to debate the subject. It does, however, offer suggestions that will, if acted on, help you on your spiritual journey.

You live in a world of multiplicity, not either or. It is a world of colour, not black and white. Enjoy the colours in your life and remember, you have more than an either or choice and keep your mind open to all possibilities.

Pursuit of Happiness

The quest for happiness is part of what makes you a human being. It is probably fair to say that most human beings seek happiness in one way or another. This part of the discussion is a reminder that happiness is of two kinds. One is temporary, the other is permanent.

Temporary happiness may occur when you go to a movie, a football game or a party. This is material happiness and will not last. Permanent happiness is something completely different. It occurs when you develop your spiritual assets rather than your spiritual liabilities.

This happiness is knowing that it is okay to be you. It is okay to live your life free of fear, guilt and shame. It is knowing that if you are willing, everything is possible. It is knowing you have something real to share with your loved ones and others. It is knowing you don't have to be perfect, just willing to try.

The Light

It would have been very easy, at the beginning of this chapter or the previous one to say, that's it, you can now rely on yourself, you don't need anything else. You have the tools, go and practise the three steps and the other suggestions, take time out, meditate and you will have peace of mind and happiness for the rest of your life.

However, that would not be true and it would be selling you short because, what you have got up to the previous chapter works only on the material side of your being. There is no guarantee that the first part of this approach, on its own, will work in the long term. There are certain types of people who may manage and survive on their own, for a time but eventually, the old self will come back and reassert itself.

Experience has shown that those who think they are the source of their own power and light will, sooner or later, end up in the dark. This is because human beings are dependent beings, they need the power of the light but the light won't go on by itself – you have to switch it on. The question is, how do you switch on this light? The simple answer is, prayer.

Prayer

Prayer is the master switch. If you are not familiar with prayer, simply say, "O God, show me the way." If you have a problem with the word God, simply say, "Help me". Remember, the power of your words is powerful.

That is it! It is that simple to pray. Then watch what happens. Continue to practise the three steps, the affirmations, time out, meditation – basically, as many of these suggestions as you can. All of these actions take seconds to practise, even if you do them all together, they can all be practised in much less than a minute, even the meditations can be shortened.

Remember the meditation that works best is the one that you should do whether its long or short. Likewise, what's the best approach to managing your thoughts and feelings? The answer is the one you do. What is the best prayer? The one you say. You get the idea!

Practise as many of the exercises in this book every day, as you go through your routine. Keep the practices short and regular for best results.

About God – To Believe or Not to Believe

So, you don't believe in God! But are you sure there is no such being? Belief is a strange idea. It implies an element of doubt. How is it that you are willing to place your well-being on something that may or may not be true? What if there is a God? It certainly has not been disproved.

You are certainly entitled to your belief or unbelief but, what if your unbelief is wrong? Throughout history, human beings have believed in many things that later turned out to be incorrect.

Believing or not believing in something does not make it true or false. Of course, human beings love to have something to believe in. It is a fundamental need but right now in the history of humanity, it is actually possible to know if God exists.

Remember, knowing is different from believing and the time has come to know. The only way to know is to investigate for yourself. If you leave this investigation to someone else, you will never know and you will always be in doubt.

Knowing, Thinking and Believing

You may be right or you may be wrong about God. Either way, it is important to keep an open mind. There were many who laughed at those who were attempting to fly machines that were heavier than air.

How wrong they were! The Wright brothers and others had something else, other than belief. They had a knowing. They knew they could do it. They knew they could make a machine that was heavier than air that could fly. There are those who know and there are those who believe and think they know.

Knowers know they know. Believers think they know. Knowing is a condition that goes way beyond belief.

Become a Knower

To become a knower, you must be willing to search for the truth. If you seek truthful answers, you will find them.

It is not enough, in this day of information overload and fake news, to blindly accept other people's opinions of what is true or false. If you want to be informed of what is true, then you must become a seeker of truth. If you are sincere in this quest, you will be successful.

The saddest thing, in this day, is to watch intelligent human beings willingly use their intellect to spread lies and discord throughout the world. Even now, as the world heads into a new decade and battles with the latest global pandemic, any semblance of what is true is spun and twisted to such an extent that lies have become the norm.

Politicians appear to be deaf to the cries of the people for justice and fairness. Some journalists, having strayed far from investigating issues of public concern, instead pander to whatever side of the political divide their employers' support.

Energy, Power, Spirit

It is now accepted that the world is round and radio waves have always been in existence. It is not beyond the bounds of possibility to imagine that there is nothing in existence today that wasn't in existence at the time of the so-called Big Bang or, whenever the world of time began. This would mean that everything that you see today would have existed in some form or other, like energy, power or spirit, or even just a thought but, whose thought?

If every idea in the world starts with a thought, that would mean that everything already exists in an invisible realm, waiting to become visible or, waiting to be brought to the next level of its existence. This would mean that thoughts and ideas are the forerunner of everything in existence, be it a table, a planet, a star, a car or computer. It is not too much of a stretch for the intellect of mankind to realise the necessity for the existence of powers greater than the material world of humanity and even the universe itself.

This kind of thinking may appear to be a bit too far outside the box for some but, it is absolutely necessary for you to open your mind and expand your thinking if you are to have contentment in your life.

A Concept of God

Spirituality and peace of mind are ultimately about being aware of that part of you that makes you human. It involves living a way of life based on the values of the community that you live in and most of all, the values you set for yourself. This is what will bring happiness, peace of mind and overall well-being into your life.

As mentioned earlier organised religion may or may not be a part of your spiritual journey. There are those who find some form of religion most beneficial however, even within a religious setting, you will still have to maintain your own spirituality and live within the boundaries of the values you set for yourself.

Awakening spiritually will, eventually, necessitate the inclusion of a concept of God, with or without a religious connection. Doing some investigation of the established religions will inform you of the different concepts people hold.

If you do not already have a concept of God, then your religious investigation will help you along. If you want peace of mind, happiness and a greater sense of wellbeing permanently in your life, keep your mind open to all options. For more in-depth discussions on many of the topics in this chapter check out *Some Answered Questions* by Abdul Baha. See reading list – Inspiring Books on page 280.

CHAPTER TWENTY-TWO

Concluding Thoughts

In the first couple of chapters, you were introduced to a three-step approach to managing troublesome feelings, attitudes, thoughts and emotions (FATE) as a pathway to happiness and peace of mind. Throughout the rest of this book you were introduced to other ideas and suggestions, to further help you on your way. As you begin the final chapter, you have come a long way. You now have the essential tools you need to bring lasting happiness and peace of mind into your life permanently and continue your development.

If you have been practising the steps and the other suggestions, you are well on your way to greater wellbeing and real happiness by now. If you have just read through these pages and not practised on the way that's okay too. However, it is time for you to begin your practice because knowing how to do something is of little use to you unless you actually do it.

Now that you know how it all works, with a little regular practice, you will quickly find contentment coming into your life. The simplest way to approach this is to go to the quick guide and work your way through the steps first. Then, gradually introduce the rest of the suggestions into your life.

There is No End

Although this is the concluding chapter it is far from the end. This is because your evolution towards happiness and well-being is a journey that has no final destination.

This means your progress is unlimited. So, instead of this chapter being a conclusion, it contains some additional thoughts and suggestions that you may find helpful as you continue your journey. One of these additions is of primary importance and it is to remind you again that when it comes to your own well-being you must put yourself first. In other words do it for yourself and not for someone else.

The reality is that if you are working on your own well-being just because someone else wants you to the changes you make in your life will not be permanent. If you do this you will be allowing another person to decide if and when you can have peace and contentment in your life! This is far too important a matter to place in the hands of someone else.

On the other hand if you are developing your well-being for yourself the changes you make will be permanent, at least until you decide you want to go back to being miserable. Hopefully, you will never make that decision. When you take responsibility for your own well-being lasting peace of mind and contentment will come into your life then you will have something very special to share with others.

Remember, this is all about managing your own thoughts and feelings not about managing how other people think and feel about you. Take care of yourself first, so that you are able to take care of your loved ones. The practice of this suggestion will have positive effects in all your relationships this is simply because if you don't love and care for yourself you will never be able to love and care for anyone else.

Bit by Bit

Keep this book close and as time goes by read a few paragraphs now and then, every day if possible. This will keep you reminded that your personal well-being needs regular attention. When you are new to this process, you may need to consciously attend to your well-being on an hourly basis, maybe even on a moment-to-moment basis but this will depend on your own personal needs.

As you continue to practise the suggestions and your awareness increases, you will find that you are starting to take care of your well-being needs spontaneously. You will gradually start to take over responsibility for your own peace of mind and contentment as you grow in confidence.

Bit by bit, you will become aware that much of your well-being is being taken care of at times when you are not even conscious of it, such as when you are asleep, at work or at play. During other times you will consciously take on the responsibility of managing your thoughts and feelings and will eventually come to realise that you are creating your own peace of mind and happiness.

Information and Knowledge

This is a lifelong, life-changing process and there is quite a bit of information in these pages nevertheless the whole process remains easy to learn and simple to use. The simplicity remains the same as days turn into weeks and months into years. What changes is your perception and understanding of what life is really all about as you begin to grow in wisdom and confidence. If the three steps and at least some of the other suggestions are applied regularly, over a sustained period of time, your life will be transformed.

To continue to grow and develop your overall well-being you will need material and spiritual knowledge. In this case, knowledge is much more than information. This kind of knowledge will come from the practice of this approach and any other approach that takes on board the need to foster material as well as spiritual development. This kind of knowledge is a knowing, not just a belief, that all is well in your world at all times and under all conditions.

There was probably a time in your life when you were happy enough to believe in something because somebody else said it was true. but this kind of second-hand belief system is no longer enough to satisfy the needs of a more vulnerable and in some ways more advanced humanity. There have been many examples throughout the history of humanity when people believed in something that later turned out to be untrue, for example, the belief that the world was flat. The time has come for you to move to the next level of being, the level of knowing. However, you can only reach this level of being through your own willingness to change, the practice of this or a similar approach to well-being and your own search for what is true.

Short Meditations

When first introduced to meditation many people commit too much time. They show great enthusiasm for the first couple of weeks but this quickly fizzles out. When the first signs of resistance show up, they find it difficult to keep going. Unfortunately, this usually ends up with no meditation being practised at all. When you first begin to practice the meditations in this book, keep your meditations short, especially if you are completely new to the practice.

Start by meditating for no more than a few minutes at a time. The practice of "time out" is ideally suited for beginners and those who want to get back into meditation. Practise short meditations until you actually begin to enjoy and look forward to those peaceful moments.

After a couple of months, try adding a longer meditation once a week; maybe a fifteen-minute meditation. The idea here is to gradually introduce meditation into your life. You can always increase the length of your meditations but if you stop altogether, it will be difficult to get started again. So, when you are new keep it short and regular. Commit to the minimum but do a little bit more.

Nothing New

This approach to well-being, is not necessarily new. It has been presented in many different formats ever since human beings could think, feel and communicate. It is set out, in this text, with a core of three simple steps. The other suggestions are in effect, an expansion of these three core steps. The reason for this is to keep it as user friendly as possible: in other words, "easy to learn and simple to use".

Although there are a lot of suggestions and ideas to reflect on, believe it or not, this is really one of the simplest approaches to managing thoughts and feelings that actually works. Introduce the ideas gradually into your life and you will find that they fit perfectly into your day.

All the concepts and suggestions here are compatible with whatever therapeutic remedies you may be already using. To this end the motto of this programme is "as well as never instead of".

Uncomplicated Approach

The idea of finding and developing an uncomplicated approach to managing thoughts and feelings that actually works goes back more than three decades. The core workings are set out in these pages, first in a very simple, easy-to-learn format then later, in greater detail.

You will not need the detail when you first begin using the core steps and suggestions. However, as you make progress, you will need to become more familiar with the finer points of the process if you wish to enjoy continuous peace of mind and happiness.

Not Much has Changed

In the thirty years or so since the beginnings of this work, things haven't changed all that much in relation to real solutions to the problem of troublesome thoughts and feelings. Yes, there has been research but still, there appears to be very little on offer by way of real solutions to address mental health issues, brought about by the conditions and environment in which people find themselves.

Statistics show that the problems of unhappiness, anxiety, stress, drug addiction, alcoholism, suicides and so on are all on the increase. Yes, there is psychotherapy, counselling and medication but even the ones that work in the long term, are not available to everyone.

The Solution Has Become the Problem

It has reached such a crisis point in many places, the world over, that some of the solutions have actually become the problem. For example, research has shown that the use of prescription medicines to tackle anxiety and depression, in both the USA and the UK, has been increasing at an alarming rate for a number of years.

You do not need to be part of this statistic. If you are troubled by thoughts and feelings, you can change using this approach.

You do not have to be troubled by thoughts and feelings to get something from this book. No matter what your mental state, you can always improve on it. One of the best ways to protect your own mental health is to learn how to manage your own thoughts and feelings. This is also the key to contentment and lasting peace of mind.

An additional benefit of using this approach is that once you know how to apply it in your own life, you will have something of real value to pass on to others.

It Works and It's Simple

Human beings have a tendency towards over complication and this can sometimes prevent people from even trying something new. This is why, at the beginning of this book, the core steps are set out as simply as possible, for you to practise immediately on any kind of thought or feeling.

The other suggestions are also simple and can be learned in minutes and practised in seconds. The discussions throughout the book will obviously take a bit longer to get your head around but stick with it and it will be worth it. Remember, the practices are simple and they work.

It is important to remember this and not let its perceived complications or simplicity fool you. This would be the classic mistake. If you haven't tried this approach, you cannot make an informed decision on whether it works or not. Making a judgement on anything without trying it first will keep you in permanent ignorance.

To simplify the learning process first commit the three steps in Chapter 2 to memory next, learn how to practise Time Out you will find this on Chapter 14. To memorise these two exercises will take just a few minutes. You will be able to consolidate your learning by practising them as many times as you can each day. Then gradually work as many of the other exercises as you can into your life.

The difficulty with this approach is not in knowing what you have to do but, in actually doing it. Simplicity does not mean easy although the practices are both simple and easy. The trouble may be in coming to terms with why you need to take certain actions to get a particular result. This will take a bit of getting used to. The understanding will come through practice.

Your Decision

If you decide to use this approach and keep applying it, your life will change. You will begin to sense your life in a new and wonderful way. You will discover how to manage your own thoughts and feelings, which is the key to achieving any level of happiness and peace of mind.

Remember that feelings, attitudes, thoughts and emotions are central to every activity and behaviour you will ever participate in. How you manage these constantly changing moods and conditions determine the level of well-being, happiness and peace of mind you will have in your life.

Troublesome thoughts and feelings are the greatest barrier to happiness and peace of mind for all human beings. If you apply the three core steps, as suggested, you will get relief and if you use the other suggestions along with the steps, you will be transformed. Furthermore if you can find enough humility to ask God for help, your spirit will awaken and you will know peace of mind and lasting happiness. Nobody can do this for you, you must do it for yourself. These steps work but you have to do the walking.

Inspiring Books

If you are open-minded and willing, you will find inspiration in everything you do, in every voice you hear and every word you read. The motivation to write this book has come from many sources among them real life experiences and the following reading list. Hopefully, you too can find the inspiration and willingness to start your own journey, if you haven't already. The list is just a sample of the books you can turn to for inspiration and guidance.

All or any of these books can be an invaluable resource to have close at hand, when you are in need of encouragement and guidance. In your local library and bookshops, you will also find helpful, interesting personal development materials, such as CDs and DVDs. Of course, you must apply the knowledge and information that you discover, no matter where it comes from. Remember, knowledge is useless unless it is applied.

The Bhagavad Gita (second edition, revised and enlarged). 29th printing. India.

The Book of Certitude. Wilmette, Illinois, USA. 2003.

The New Jerusalem Bible (pocket edition). Darton Longman & Todd Ltd, London. 1990.

NLP The New Technology of Achievement by **Steve Andreas** and **Charles Faulkner**. NB Publishing, London. 2003.

Some Answered Questions by **Abdul Baha**. English translation of Laura Clifford Barney by Kegan Paul, Trench. Trübner & Co., London. 1908.

Autogenic Therapy: Self-help for Mind and Body by **Jane Bird** and **Christine Pinch**. New Leaf, Gill and Macmillan, Ireland. 2002.

The Holy Bible (King James Version). Thomas Nelson, Nashville Tennessee 37214 USA, 2018.

Home Coming: Reclaiming and Championing Your Inner Child by **John Bradshaw**. Bantam Books, USA and Canada. 1990.

The Quran: A New Translation by **Tomas Cleary**. Starlatch Press, USA.

The Alchemist by **Paulo Coelho**. HarperCollins, USA. 1988.

The Power of Intention by **Wayne Dyer**. Hay House, USA. 2004.

There is a Spiritual Solution for Every Problem by **Wayne Dyer**. Thorsons, London. 2002

Living the Wisdom of the Tao by **Wayne Dyer**. Hay House, USA. 2008.

Wishes Fulfilled by **Wayne Dyer**. Hay House, USA. 2013.

Mindfulness on the Go by **Padraig O'Morain**. Hodder & Stoughton, London. 2015.

The Power of Now by **Eckhart Tolle**. New World Library, USA. 2004.

You Can Heal Your Life by **Louise L. Hay**. Eden Grove Editions, Great Britain. 1988.

Life! Reflections on Your Journey by **Louise L. Hay**. Hay House, USA. 1996.

Feel the Fear and Do It Anyway by **Susan Jeffers**. Vermillion, London.

The Power of Positive Thinking by **Norman Vincent Peale**. Vermillion, London.

The Road Less Travelled by **Scott Peck**. Simon and Shuster, USA. 1978.

The Legend of Bagger Vance by **Steven Pressfield**. Avon Books, USA. 1995.

Course in Miracles (combined volume) by **Helen Schucman** and **William T. Thetford**. Viking Penguin, USA. 1996.

The Game of Life and How to Play It by **Florence Scovel Shinn**. Vermillion, London. 2005.

Dialectical Materialism (Chapter 3. The Material and the Spiritual) by **Alexander Spirkin**. Progress Publishers, 1983

Closer Than Your Life Vein by **Henry A. Weil**. NSA, Alaska, USA. 1978.

Index

About the Author

Mattie Slattery was born and grew up in Clarecastle, a village in County Clare in the mid-west of Ireland. He is one of ten children, many loved ones, a father and grandfather. His childhood was uneventful, other than what was common to most children growing up in Ireland in the late nineteen fifties and sixties.

His work life began in his very early teens and it was at this time that he became aware of the need to be able to change and adapt to the challenges of the material world. His life experience has led him to a way of living that has evolved into the guide to peace and contentment described in this book.

Contact details:

Website: mattieslattery.com
e-Mail: mattie@mattieslattery.com

Printed in Great Britain
by Amazon